Shanghai Remembrance

Frank T. Leo

with

Joanne Parrent

James Deely

Noble House
Baltimore, Maryland

Shangai Remembrance

Copyright © 2000 Frank T. Leo

Library of Congress
Cataloging in Publication Data
ISBN 1-56167-596-2

Library of Congress Card Catalog Number:
00-101991

Published by

8019 Belair Road, Suite 10
Baltimore, Maryland 21236

Manufactured in the United States of America

To Zee and Ada

ACKNOWLEDGEMENTS

I am deeply indebted to all my friends who helped me in writing this book. The origin of the work is family histories, first hand accounts, and conversations with my mother, other relatives, and family members. These were first assembled as a lengthy collection of weekly after dinner dialogues taped by my dear friend Nikki Deloffre. These were then transcribed by her, resulting in a thick volume of disconnected anecdotes. An enormous thanks to Nikki for her part in kick starting the program.

James Deely, my best friend, brought his special gift of story telling to the book. For over a year, he helped me weave the volume into a cohesive and detailed chronicle. His style and acute visual sense are an important part of the finished work. A sincere thank you for bringing my story to life.

The next acknowledgement goes to Lucy Scriveri who transcribed my handwritten work on to a computer disk.

Joanne Parrent, an established writer, brought her polished and professional skills to the manuscript.

Loyal friends including Beverly Trupp, Bill Krim, Yolanda Landrum, and Andrea Anderson gave me the gift of encouragement and emotional support throughout the years. I am forever grateful to them.

Finally, the most heartfelt acknowledgement to all those not mentioned who played a role in this family history.

INTRODUCTION

The world into which I was born, an aristocratic family from Changchow, China, was a world steeped in tradition. The history of my family for 19 generations, going back 300 years, had been handwritten on rice paper and then carefully bound with silk threads into volumes about two inches thick. These volumes, which were kept in cedar chests, were among my family's most treasured possessions. By the time I was born, there were four tall stacks of books, each about three feet high. The oldest of these manuscripts, which were written in an ancient prose using ancient characters, recounted stories from the lives of my ancestors, many of whom from the earliest days of the Ching Dynasty, had held high positions in the Imperial Court.

I was about five years old when I first remember looking at the books. The Japanese invasion of China in 1937 had destroyed our ancestral home in Changchow and forced my family to flee Shanghai. The books were among the few precious possessions my father was able to save from the destruction. When my parents and my uncle discovered that some of the rice paper volumes were starting to deteriorate, my father spared no expense in hiring two venerable scholars, with long flowing white beards, to decipher the books and copy all of them onto new pages, in calligraphy.

The manuscripts had been written by each son, who, according to tradition, after his father's death, would record the life achievements of his father and the birth of each child. My grandfather had died some years earlier and it was time for my father to pen his father's biography and also record my birth and that of my sister.

Three decades later, in Shanghai in January, 1966, my father died. Though many of my ancestors had lived long lives, into their eighties and nineties, my father was just sixty-one when he was stricken with a fatal heart attack. Six months after his death, in June, 1966, the Cultural Revolution began in China. Gangs of youths, calling themselves Red Guards, went through neighborhoods, block by block, ransacking homes and robbing the inhabitants. They carried out into the streets every reminder of a Capitalist past or symbol of a bourgeois life style—including books and photos—and burned them. During this devastating period, more people died than had in the eight-year war with Japan. Many of the deaths were the result of suicides by those unable to withstand the physical and mental torture inflicted by the mobs of Red Guards. Included among those were my mother's sister, Aunt Dan-Yee and her husband, my Uncle Soong, who committed suicide together.

When the Cultural Revolution began, my mother was in Hong Kong. She had fled to that then-British colony in 1952 in order to help her only son fulfill his dreams. Every year since, she returned to China to live with my father in Shanghai but stayed only long enough—six months at the beginning and nine months later—to be able to get an exit visa and return to Hong Kong. After my father died, my mother planned to continue to split her time between the two cities. Fortunately, she was in Hong Kong when the Cultural Revolution began and didn't return to China for another twelve years, until that violent period finally ended. The apartment which my father lived in at the time of his death was still occupied by Mamma Chang, my beloved former nanny, who had lived with our family since I was a very small child, and Mamma Chang's niece, Jade.

During the Cultural Revolution, my father's apartment was ransacked many times. Mamma Chang and Jade were harassed and tormented. Most of their belongings, as well as those of my parents, were confiscated or destroyed. One quilt and one change of clothes each were all that Mamma Chang and Jade were allowed to keep after the numerous raids. Already old and sick, Mamma Chang could not endure the cold winter and extreme deprivation. She died, and Jade succumbed shortly thereafter.

One night, in the midst of these attacks, the precious volumes of family history, so carefully preserved for 350 years and then restored by my father and uncle, were seized by Red Guards, thrown on a bonfire and burned.

The Cultural Revolution finally ended in 1976. The infamous "Gang of Four"—as the leaders of the movement were called—were imprisoned and a new China emerged. At the urging of my mother, I visited China in 1980, the first time I was able to return to my homeland in twenty-seven years. Seeing Shanghai again, where I grew up in the time spanning the war with the Japanese, the Second World War and the civil war which led to Mao's communist regime, I was flooded with memories of my childhood. I realized that my parents were the last survivors of a way of life in China which has now vanished as violently as the destruction of the books which recorded that way of life. But, though the handwritten family histories had been destroyed, the memories of my mother, myself and other friends and relatives had not. As I observed the new China, different from both my past and from my present American life, I decided that it was time for me, the representative of the 20th generation of my family, to write the last volume. Unlike in the past, it would be typed on a computer, rather than handwritten on rice paper. Also, unlike in the past, it would not be only my father's life and achievements, but my mother's as well. To my father and his ancestors I owe the ancient tradition of our past, but to my mother, a modern woman by China's standards in the first half of the twentieth century and a bridge to my future, I owe my freedom. This remembrance will be her story as well as my own, shored up by her courage and filled with her vivid memories of Shanghai.

Part One:
Changchow

Chapter One _____

" This baby had to have been a saint for nine lifetimes to reincarnate as my grandson," Grandfather Liu mused to himself on the day I was born. "He will be the center of the universe. The sun and moon will surely rotate around him." The day of that lucky reincarnation was a hot August morning in 1935, in Changchow, China. Even though it was only ten a.m., the temperature was already hovering close to ninety degrees. The cicadas, from their perch in the willow trees, droned on in a one note symphony. Reed blinds, mounted on the eaves outside the windows for the summer season, were rolled down to keep the rooms in the vast compound dark and cool. Nevertheless, the air was still and it was hot and humid inside. In a large bedroom, my mother, Ada, was lying on an oversized brass bed in the midst of a difficult labor, which had begun the night before. A woman servant sitting next to the big brass bed gently waved a palm fan at my mother's sweat-drenched face. Periodically, the servant leaned over to blot the perspiration from her forehead with a small damp towel. A midwife waited with several other servants near the bed. At the other end of the room, in a sitting area, a half dozen female relatives from my father's side of the family sipped cool drinks. They chatted in low voices while fanning themselves with sandalwood fans. Finally, the time came. Everyone rose and moved toward the bed, watching silently as I entered the world. The midwife quickly announced that I was male and the chatter, now in a more excited tone, started up again. A servant woman dashed out of the bedroom and ran to my Grandfather Liu's quarters. My father, Zee, and his younger brother, Chi, were both with Grandfather Liu awaiting the news. Grandfather, elated over the announcement that his son and daughter-in-law had produced a male heir, immediately ordered that the family shrine be opened to give thanks for this momentous event. A servant was sent full speed from Grandfather's quarters through several courtyards and buildings to the shrine, shouting, "Old Master orders that the shrine be opened. It's a boy!"

A distant relative of our family was in charge of the shrine. A devout Buddhist who would only eat vegetarian meals which were specially prepared in the kitchen with separate utensils, she was called by everyone, "Miss Vegetarian". From an early age, she had devoted her life to Buddha, and Grandfather had given her accommodations on the compound, adjacent to the shrine building. Her duties included daily candle lighting and burning of incense in the shrine. She also chanted regularly, imploring Buddha and the ancestors to protect the family. At the time of major holidays, festivals, birthdays, deaths, and sicknesses, the family expected her to intensify her chants. My birth was the most important event in Miss Vegetarian's career. She began chanting prayers the day my mother's pregnancy was announced and, as the birth drew near, her chanting grew to a frenzy. She would chant for hours, kneeling in the shrine amidst hundreds of glowing red candles, completely enveloped in a cloud of incense smoke.

At the announcement of my birth, an army of servants under Miss Vegetarian's direction went into expert action to prepare the shrine. Within minutes, the large square rosewood table in front of the altar was set with many place settings for the spirits of the ancestors. The side of the table facing the entrance to the shrine was draped with a red satin panel, which was covered with elaborate embroidery. Along the middle top edge of the panel, an incense burner was placed, with wrist-sized red candles burning on each side of it. A round kneeling pad about a foot thick was placed on the floor in front of the satin panel. Six huge arm chairs, two on each side, were placed on the other three sides of the table. There were at least four or five place settings in front of each set of two chairs—the spirits of the ancestors apparently do not occupy the same physical space as mortals. From the kitchen, trays of piping hot banquet food were brought in, filling the center of the table.

Announced by his man servant preceding him, the Old Master arrived at the Shrine. For this special occasion, the double center gates of the shrine were opened and Miss Vegetarian stood at the gate with her head bowed in respect. She had on her finest cotton robe, since a devout Buddhist never wore silk. Grandpa, eighty-six years old, tread in a very slow gait with two handmaidens supporting him. Behind him, in a long line, were my father, uncle, aunts, birthing witnesses and other family members, as well as a contingent of men and women servants. Once inside, Grandpa knelt down on the kneeling pad and formally kowtowed three times. As he rose, a chair was brought over for him. He sat in it and watched as the seventy-five plus family members each, one by one, took their turn in this ritual, in order of their ranking. Even Grandfather's third and last remaining wife, known as Mrs. Upstairs because she rarely ventured downstairs from her bedroom suite on an upper floor, came downstairs for this most special event. She was the leader of the female contingent of the family, which followed the last male family member in the cortege.

Grandfather had a jubilant feeling as he watched the procession. He was now completely satisfied that this daughter-in-law had indeed been a good choice. In the tradition of the time, only a male heir could inherit the family fortune, and he was very happy to at last have a male heir. He had predicted the birth of a boy as soon as the bride of four months announced her pregnancy. Stroking his long white beard, he took pride in his farsightedness and modern thinking in approving his son's marriage, the first marriage of choice ever in the family. In the past, all marriages had been arranged by parents, and the bride and groom usually met each other for the first time on their wedding night. Grandfather remembered that, when this wedding announcement was made, many Changchow fathers were very indignant. How could the son of a prominent family be allowed to choose such an outrageously modern girl as a wife? She was schooled in Shanghai and lived her life as she pleased, without parental control. It seemed to these community fathers that any of a number of local girls from good families would have been far better choices. The general consensus was that Old Master Liu had made a terrible mistake by letting his son choose his own wife.

Even many of the relatives who lived in the family compound secretly had hoped that Grandfather's oldest son, Zee, my father, would continue to disappoint his father. He had been a college dropout, an opium addict and frequenter of many of the town brothels. Some of these relatives hoped to be able to seize control of the vast family fortune if the new bride did not produce a male heir before the Old Master died. A rumor circulated the town and the family compound that this modern girl had had a hysterectomy in her youth, so she could never produce an heir, male or otherwise. When her pregnancy was announced, more rumors started to fly. One claimed the pregnancy was false and that a pregnant peasant woman was hidden in the compound, whose newborn would be proclaimed as the heir. Others said that the pregnancy could be real but several other pregnant women were hidden out of sight. If the bride delivered a girl, there surely would be a boy among the other mothers. A quick switch would protect the inheritance. Grandfather ignored the rumors, confident that this child would be a boy. To prevent any later squabble as to the birth circumstance and subsequent inheritance, however, he masterminded the setting of the birth, making sure that several key eye witnesses were present.

As he sat in the shrine watching the family thank the ancestors for the new baby boy, he was content. This child would ensure that the ancient family traditions and the family fortune would be safe and secure. At that blissful moment in front of the family shrine, he could not possibly imagine the profound upheaval and change which would overtake both his family and his ancient homeland during the next two decades.

Chapter Two

Grandfather Liu came from a long line of officials who held high positions in the Imperial Court, from as far back as the early days of the Ching Dynasty, in the 17th century. One of our family ancestors had even been married to the favorite daughter of an Emperor. He was chosen by the Emperor over other highly placed officials because of his good looks, intelligence and skills to be the consort to the princess. When my father told me stories about my ancestors as a child, he was particularly proud of this one who had brought royal blood to our lineage.

Another ancestor worked his way up to being Prime Minister, the highest position in the Imperial Court. He served the then Emperor for many years, finally retiring to his ancestral home in Changchow. When the Emperor was dying, however, he asked the retired Prime Minister to return to court to assist his teenage son in ruling the kingdom. The Prime Minister who had succeeded the retired man, was his nephew. When the Emperor died, the older man returned to court and he and his nephew both served the young Emperor as the Left Prime Minister and the Right Prime Minister. It was an extremely rare and honored distinction for the two Imperial Court Prime Ministers to be from the same family.

The old Prime Minister served for many more years until the Emperor had become an adult with a son of his own. Then, one day in the midst of a briefing, this ancestor had a stroke and died in the presence of the Emperor. The grief stricken Emperor commanded his son, the Crown Prince, to accompany the Prime Minister's body back to his home town, Changchow. It is approximately eight hundred miles between the Imperial Palace in Peking and Changchow, and the Emperor ordered that the roadway along the entire distance be covered with golden sand in tribute to my ancestor. The funeral cortege then traveled on foot along this golden road, led by the young Crown Prince, on horseback.

Another ancestor, though also intelligent and hard working, was not as lucky in his dealings with the Imperial Court. He had a serious eyesight problem and, of course, he lived in an age before eyeglasses became commonplace. My parents, as they told his sad tale, assumed that his problem must have been nearsightedness. Over a period of years this industrious man was rewarded with higher and higher ranking in the Imperial Court until he finally achieved a position lofty enough to join those of equally esteemed rank in the daily audience with the Emperor. Each day at dawn, the Emperor would sit on his throne with his highest officials standing, in order of their rank, below the many marble steps that led to the throne. If an official had important business to conduct with the Emperor, he approached the throne, walking up the countless marble steps with his body bowed low and eyes cast downward. When he was dismissed, he had to retreat in the same manner, backing down the steps. All officials wore long silk robes with intricate brocade and knee length ropes made of beads, often jade, agate or carved ivory. In summer, the robes were thin silk. In winter, heavy silk robes were lined in fur—sable, fox or wolf depending on your rank—to protect against the icy chill that captured the wide inner courtyards of the Forbidden City.

One day this ancestor with poor eyesight was beckoned to approach the Emperor. As he moved up the steps, in the proper bowing posture, his bead rope caught on the tip of his boot. The silken cord which connected the carved beads snapped and, instantly, all the beads were cast in disarray. He was horrified at having committed this terrible breech of etiquette. The rules of the court were ancient and precise, however, so whatever the excuse, his punishment was the traditional demotion of three ranks. Nearly a lifetime of devotion to the throne was suddenly dissipated, like the beads, in a hundred directions. After his demotion, this nearsighted ancestor was no longer in a ranking high enough to be present in court, but with an energy common to many generations of my family, he again worked hard and moved back up the ranks. Once again, he achieved that most esteemed position and was allowed to present himself at dawn before the Emperor. But, once again it happened. His poor eyesight caused him to stumble up the marble steps, and his silk rope broke, scattering the beads. Again he was demoted, but again he worked to regain his position. On his third attempt to appear before the Emperor on the marble steps, the beads broke for the last time. Now an old man, he was broken, his dreams and ambitions never to be realized. In spite of his ability and dedication, he was forever among those who did not attain an audience with the Emperor. Grandfather Liu, unlike so many of these ancestors, was not politically ambitious. The third of six brothers, he was born in 1849 in his hometown, Changchow, and was recorded as the eighteenth generation in the family history books. He was the lowest ranked official in our family history, never attempting to achieve a position in the Imperial Court in Peking. For a brief time, he did hold a political position in his local town of Changchow, but his real talent lay elsewhere.

Grandpa retired from local politics by the turn of the century and turned his energy into several business ventures. His father backed him with a large amount of capital and, in a short span of time, he amassed a fortune. Bright and aggressive, he soon became the controller of all the family finances and his father's most favorite, capable and trusted son. Three of his brothers had died fairly early in life and the two remaining brothers had little ambition in either politics or business. Content with their inherited wealth, they married, had children and lived a life of leisure. Unlike his brothers, Grandpa was very interested in both continued financial success and the legacy he would leave behind. He acquired large tracts of land which adjoined the existing household and greatly expanded the family compound. He built a perimeter wall surrounding the entire property, making the compound like a small walled city. Each brother then built his own house on the compound, with separate entrance gates through the outer wall. Grandpa moved into the main residence, which had been previously occupied by his now deceased father. Creating a residence uniquely impressive for that part of the world, he remodeled and expanded the building. A pair of bright red doors in the main gate to the compound, eight foot wide by ten foot high, opened into his residence. In the center of each door was a large brass lion's head with a brass ring in its mouth. To each side there were smaller doors for everyday use. Inside the gates was a stone paved courtyard, leading to a large center hall. At the back of the hall, was another gate with another pair of lacquered doors and smaller doors on the sides. This second gate opened to a sunken courtyard, with a covered colonnade on four sides, surrounded by carved wood railings and decorated with potted plants, which were changed each season. Another center hall was across from it and off the hall on each side were smaller rooms, their doors opening to the colonnade. The same setting repeated ten times, with ten sets of center gates designed in a straight line from south to north. After the sixth courtyard, the scale of the interior rooms got larger and the sleeping quarters on the sides rose to two stories. All the rooms were furnished with carved Chinese rosewood furniture.

Most guests would be escorted on foot through the enormous length of the building complex. A VIP visitor would be allowed to remain in his personal sedan chair through the ten sets of opened gates. In the distance, Grandpa, seated in the tenth central hall, awaited his guest, making an unforgettable impression on even the most important of visitors.

Instead of dividing the estate after their father's death, Grandpa and his brothers remained as one financial unit with Grandpa at the helm of the family empire. The business ventures Grandpa engaged in were all remarkably successful. His holdings included a plant which processed newly harvested rice from the family's rice lands, a factory which manufactured soy sauce and a chain of pawn shops. His major investments, however, were in textiles and banking. Entrepreneurs who needed capital for business ventures often came to Grandpa. If he thought the plan was sound and the men were capable and reliable, he would not hesitate to become a backer, often investing large sums in new companies. His wisdom and Midas touch made nearly every venture a profitable one.

In the early 1900s, Shanghai, approximately 280 miles east of Changchow, was the busiest seaport in Asia and was developing into an international business center. One day, a man from Shanghai came to Grandpa, hoping to raise capital for a spinning mill in Shanghai, which would spin raw cotton into spools of thread. Grandpa's brothers didn't want to make this investment, claiming the company was too far away to control. Grandpa, however, decided to bankroll the operation with his personal money, and it soon became one of the most successful textile businesses in southeast Asia. This particular investment, in "Success Textiles," would help our family make it through the difficult years to come.

Grandfather's success in his personal goals, however, did not come as easily or as quickly as his business success. In the custom of the times, his parents had arranged a marriage for him when he was nineteen years old. His fiancee was a woman from a local prominent family much like his own. Two years after the marriage, in 1870, she produced a son. The happy event was marred, however, with the news that the child was retarded. Little was understood about the mind in those days and everyone thought that the boy was crazy. Whether crazy or retarded, when he reached the age of twenty, as the first born son from an eminent and powerful family, there were no shortage of matchmakers who came to present young girls as potential wives. He married a woman who was selected for him and she bore a son the following year. Shortly after his child's birth, the retarded man died. Grandpa, who had never been fond of his son, was also not fond of his grandson, and didn't consider him an appropriate heir.

In Changchow then, there were numerous brothels, and Grandpa, like other wealthy men during those times, often patronized the top-level establishments. The most exclusive brothels were housed in beautifully furnished mansions, with bedroom wings three stories high and dozens of bedrooms on every floor. Each night, banquets were held in the most formal of settings and, during the meal, the gentlemen guests were entertained by singers and dancers. The working girls were purchased by the Madam when they were only six or seven years old. Many poor families from rural areas sold their pretty young daughters to brothels, giving the family one less mouth to feed, as well as instant cash. When a child entered a brothel, she immediately began intensive training in how to please future clients. The young girls were taught literature and ink wash painting, as well as how to play musical instruments and chess. Depending on their aptitude, they were also instructed in singing, dancing and poetry. While in training, the girls' duties included the household chores and waiting on the older girls, who spent most of their time receiving customers. These children, according to rumor, were also fed an herb concoction which would render them sterile for life. When a girl reached her sixteenth birthday, she began to take in clients. The highest bidder at an in-house auction had the privilege of deflowering the virgin. Many patrons would eye a particular young girl for years and anxiously await the day she would be offered to the highest bidder. A client also could purchase a girl at any time and bring her into his household as a concubine.

Grandpa visited the best of these establishments on a regular basis, and, in time, purchased two young girls to take home as Wife No. 2 and Wife No. 3. Neither of these young women were able to bear children, however, and Grandpa wanted children, especially sons. A matchmaker eventually learned of Grandpa's desire and presented him with an appropriate choice. The potential bride was from an educated but poor family. Large-boned and tall, she definitely didn't meet the standard of petite beauty, which was common in those days. Some said she was a handsome woman but, since she was over twenty and not yet betrothed, she was considered almost an old maid. Nevertheless, the deal was struck and, in 1902, she became Wife No. 4 to Grandpa, thirty-five years her senior. In the first three years of the marriage, she produced three children in rapid succession. The first two were girls, and were always later addressed as, "Miss No. 1" and "Miss No. 2." The third child, born in December 1905, was a boy, "Zee." He was my father. Eight years later, in 1913, my Grandmother delivered a second son, my Uncle "Chi."

The four pregnancies added considerable girth to Grandma's already bigger than usual frame. After the last baby, she was quite a large plump woman. Grandpa still had a roving eye and, of course, an inexhaustible cash supply. In his late sixties, he bought four more girls from the brothels and added luxury quarters for these hand-picked concubines. Each of these new brides were allotted ten handmaidens, as well as several women servants. Servants were usually peasant women, hired to do all the household chores, while handmaidens were slaves, purchased at the same age as the girls who were sold to brothels. Most parents would rather sell a child to a wealthy household than to a brothel, so the brightest and prettiest girls were always first available to families like ours. A few generations before Grandpa, the tradition of slavery in our family was equated as an act of charity. Unlike the common practice, the girls were never expected to do heavy work. Their main duties were to keep the mistress company, comb her hair, pour tea, help her get dressed, etc. They were taught how to read and write by an old scholar who held classes within the compound walls. This same tutor taught the family children in their early years, including my father, uncle and aunts.

When a handmaiden reached marrying age, sixteen or older, she was married off in the same manner as the daughters of the family, complete with a dowry. Many local merchants sent matchmakers to inquire about the availability of these refined and pretty girls. A handmaiden from a wealthy family was considered an infinitely better choice than the only daughter of a poor family. A couple of the handmaidens in our family were exceptionally beautiful. One was seen by a local politician who was visiting Grandpa one day. The politician immediately sent a matchmaker to make the contract and soon married the girl. Later, he became the Minister of Finance in Chiang Kai-Shek's government. Another handmaiden was chosen by a well-educated widower, who was a house guest at the compound. They eventually had four sons, all of whom became medical doctors, earning advanced degrees from Johns Hopkins University in the United States. One of their sons became the personal physician to Mao Tse-Tung in the 70s, and attended Deng Xiao-Ping in the 80s. I remember both of these former handmaidens, whom I always addressed as "Aunts." Our servants treated the return visits of these aunts with the same dignity and respect as my own natural aunts. The majority of the handmaidens, however, married and went on with their new lives and husbands, losing touch with our family.

The luxury which surrounded Grandpa's many wives could not compensate for the life of extreme loneliness they lived. The last four wives were about fifty years younger than Grandpa. As in romance novels, the young and restless ones ran away, one with a man servant, another with the household bookkeeper. Grandpa's original wife and three others died of tuberculosis. Grandpa's No. 3 Wife lived the longest and remained very beautiful as she grew older. Her living quarters were in a two-story building, with her bedroom suite on the upper floor. She enjoyed sitting in her window, watching all that took place in and around the busy compound from her high vantage point. It was she who later became known as Mrs. Upstairs. My Grandmother, the plumpest of all the wives, had a difficult time climbing stairs. Her quarters were a large apartment complex on the ground level, which also housed her four children. Grandpa lived in his bachelor quarters known as "the study," where he was carefully looked after by a battalion of servants and handmaidens. The study was off limits to his wives, but he, of course, was free to visit whichever wife he cared to, at any time in their individual quarters.

By the late 1920s, Grandpa was nearing 80 years old and leading a most relaxed life, having earned a reputation as a charitable and generous man. He had constructed a five-story hospital next to the compound, which provided medical services free of charge to those in need. He also built an elementary school and high school which were free for the poor children who otherwise couldn't afford to go to school. There was no public educational system at that time and the majority of the population was illiterate.

Grandpa purchased an island in nearby Taiwu Lake, which was called "Horseshoe Island" because it was shaped like a horseshoe. He loved the island, and selected a beautiful spot on it for his final resting place. A content and happy man, his only worries were whether Zee, my father, or my Uncle Chi would ever produce a male heir for the family. Indeed, though his daughters pleased him, both of his sons gave Grandpa good cause for anxiety.

Chapter Three ─────────────

Neither of my father's two older sisters, Miss No. 1 and Miss No. 2, were considered as attractive. Both sisters took after their mother in their large-scale proportions, they also inclined to be willful and domineering. Nevertheless, they were both married off in their teens as the tradition dictated. Coincidentally, their husbands were rather small in stature. As a child, I always enjoyed the comical sight of my two aunts towering over their diminutive husbands. Miss No. 1 was the favorite of my grandparents so her husband was chosen with great care. He was a man from Nanking, who was both educated and from an aristocratic lineage. Miss No. 2, the least favorite of the children, was married to a man who was chosen strictly because of his wealth—his family had made its fortune in real estate in Shanghai. Neither of these two husbands ever worked for a living. Miss No. 1 supported her husband with her personal dowry and inheritance for all of her life. Miss No. 2 and her husband, however, lived in unsurpassed luxury off the fortune from her husband's family.

After a few years of wedded bliss, neither of the sisters had shown any sign of impending motherhood so everyone gave them advice on how to produce the coveted male heirs. They were told about a Buddhist temple on a faraway mountain, which supposedly had eating utensils with magical powers. If a barren woman came to the temple and stole one or more of these items, she would surely produce a male heir. Miss No. 1 and Miss No. 2 journeyed to the temple together, with their entourage of servants. When they arrived, they dutifully lit the candles and incense, then knelt and prayed to Buddha. After their prayers, they ordered a large vegetarian banquet for the whole group. Before they departed, each sister stole a pewter wine decanter and a pewter wine cup. The monks of the temple, fully aware of the legend and the intentions of these wealthy matrons, would look away at the right time so as not to see the ladies stuffing the loot into their handbags. The monks knew that a generous donation would be forthcoming—many hundred times more than the cost of the cheap pewter.

Another fertility legend led the two sisters to an even more remote mountain and another temple. A holy monk, who supposedly had been alone in his cell in a trance for over a hundred years, was meditating in this temple. He neither slept, ate nor drank, but had been sitting in the classic lotus position day and night for as long as anyone could remember. The legend was that if a woman entered the monk's room by herself, reached her hand into his pants and found his testicles, then she would produce a baby boy in the future. If she failed to find his testicles, she would never produce a male child. Both Miss No. 1 and Miss No. 2 made the journey to this temple with their combined household entourages. By turn, they entered the monk's room and followed the instructions given to them by the senior monk in charge. A condition of the magic working was that a woman could not speak about what happened in the cell until she was finally back home. If she broke this rule, the spell would be broken. As Miss No. 1 and Miss No. 2 returned home they could hardly control their elation. When finally able to tell their stories, both claimed that they had indeed found the testicles of the holy monk in that silent and bare cell. However farfetched this legend seemed, both sisters ended up becoming pregnant within a year of their pilgrimage. They each produced a healthy son, only three months apart. After the birth of their children, in keeping with tradition, the sisters returned to that distant Buddhist temple to offer a generous thanks for their miracle babies, born with the aid of the old monk's testicles.

Grandpa was happy about these grandsons his daughters produced, but they did not bear his family name and he was still most anxious about his two sons, Zee and Chi. My father, Zee, had begun patronizing the town brothels when he was barely sixteen years of age, enjoying the usual fare at the brothels—sex and drugs. By the time he entered a local college, he was a full fledged opium addict. After one year in college he dropped out, so Grandpa decided to put him to work in one of his fabric shops. Zee hated the job, and often skipped work to go to the brothels. His mother was upset with his behavior and whenever she heard that Zee was again at one of his regular haunts, she would track him down, leading a posse of her servants, brandishing broom and mop handles. The women would beat on the front door of the brothel where Zee was and demand that he come out. Zee took all this as a matter of course, usually making a hasty and undetected exit out of a back door to avoid confrontation with his mother. Grandma also tried hiring a prominent matchmaker to find a suitable wife for Zee, hoping that her son would stop philandering once he had a wife. Zee, however, flatly turned down every girl the matchmaker presented. The only woman he would marry, he claimed adamantly, would be one he chose himself.

My Uncle Chi was born when Grandpa was already in his sixties. As the youngest child and by far the best looking, he was definitely indulged. When he was in high school, he asked for and got a gymnasium built in the compound, with a full scale indoor basketball court. Both brothers loved horses, so a stable was built for them which housed four saddle horses. Unsatisfied with ordinary short and stubby Chinese ponies, the brothers went to Shanghai and bought four tall and graceful English hunters. An exercise ring was constructed and two grooms were hired who took up residence in the compound with their families. Their children would walk the horses in the exercise ring to dry off the animals' sweat when the brothers had returned from their vigorous rides in the country. Like his elder brother, Chi was a poor student, and his antics frustrated his mother to no end. Feeling hopeless about him, she would often retreat to a private garden and weep by a well. Her maids would rush to find Chi and ask him to beg his mother's forgiveness. She was in such a state of despair, they would say, that she would surely commit suicide by throwing herself into the well. Chi would dismiss them, saying that any worry was needless—his mother was much too fat to fit into the well. When Chi finished high school, he wanted to go to Shanghai for college. Due to his poor grades, however, very few colleges would even consider him. He begged and cried and finally softened his father's heart. To insure his son's enrollment and eventual graduation, Grandpa bought several acres of land in Shanghai and donated them to the college of Chi's choice for a new campus.

Meanwhile, Zee's appetite for girls wandered beyond the brothels, taking a homeward turn one day. He noticed one of his mother's handmaidens, who had recently blossomed into a delicate and fair beauty. She had an intriguing bubbly personality and a lighter than air quality. She enjoyed the attention of the young master and it was not very long before she announced that she was pregnant. The gossip about this scandalous incident consumed everyone in the family compound. All the servants' tongues were wagging, and it was like a plague had come upon the venerable old household. When Grandpa and Grandma finally got wind of it, Zee stayed away from home for several days, waiting for their anger to pass. The girl was not as fortunate as Zee, however. First, she was subject to a caning. Grandma reckoned that there were over a hundred handmaidens living in the compound. Why had this girl not refused the young master's advances? Did she not have any control over herself? Other handmaidens even claimed that she had lured the young master in, hoping not to be married off to some stranger in the future. After the severe caning, Grandma and Grandpa considered what to do with the girl. There was always the possibility that the unborn child would be a boy. Grandpa had wanted a grandson for so many years and this might be the answer. They decided that if the child was a boy, the handmaiden would be kept within the compound and her position would be of a concubine to Zee. If a girl, then the handmaiden would be married off through a matchmaker, but her child would be raised in the compound as the family daughter. Zee, not wanting further trouble and also not in love with the handmaiden, went along with the decision of his parents.

The lucky stars were not shining on that handmaiden the night of her child's birth in January, 1929. The baby was a girl. Soon after the birth, a matchmaker was summoned and the handmaiden was married to a rural family's son. Several families had vied for her since they knew the dowry for our family's handmaidens was always quite handsome. The baby girl stayed at Grandma's quarters and was raised with all the care and attendance anyone could ever hope for. Grandma was especially doting and indulgent since this was her first grandchild, and she soon turned the baby into a willful and spoiled child. Grandfather, because he really wanted a grandson, gave her a very masculine-sounding name, Cypress Forest. The child hated the name and, when she was older, changed it to an English name. Her new name came from a Hollywood movie, starring Joan Fontaine as the title character—Ivy. She liked the movie and the name so much that she insisted everyone address her from then on as Ivy.

My aging Grandfather was now more anxious than ever for a grandson and prayed fervently to the spirits of the departed ancestors for one. Finally, it seemed that his prayers might be answered. In 1930, Zee, at twenty-five, fell in love at first sight with a twenty-one-year-old city girl, while visiting relatives in Shanghai. At once, in the superstitious tradition of the time, Grandfather obtained for the young girl's Zodiac sign and time and date of birth, which he presented to a famed fortune teller. The fortune teller charted the future of this girl in every detail. In a meeting with Grandfather and Grandmother, the fortune teller was enthusiastic about the girl. He indicated that she had the tremendous inner power necessary to control her future husband. She had the ability to spur him on to unsurpassed success. To Grandfather, the most important part of the fortune teller's predictions was that this girl would bear a son. The fortune teller was totally certain of that— as certain as a fortune teller can be—and Grandfather and Grandmother were elated. At last a girl had come along who could tame this wild son of theirs, who could make him a success in the world of business. Best of all, she would produce a male heir for the family. This was a most favorable gift from the heavens. The ancestors must indeed be pleased. Hastily, Grandfather, now 80, and Grandmother, 45, planned a trip to Shanghai to meet this young woman who had such an important fate and who would make such a difference in the destiny of this family. The girl's name was Li Ai-dah. She anglicized it to Ada Lee.

Chapter Four ─────────────

A da Lee's father was a native of Wusi, a city in between Shanghai and Changchow south of the Yangtse River. It was in an area known for its wealth of natural resources—particularly rice, fresh water fish, and livestock. Grandpa Lee's family had a long history as merchants and he propelled himself to the top of that class, making the Lee family very well-to-do. As Zee always reminded Ada, however, there was no aristocratic lineage anywhere in her past. Grandpa Lee's first wife produced two daughters of which only one, Shan-dah, survived. He took a second wife in the hope that she would give him a son. This wife, my Grandma Lee, gave birth to a girl, Ada, in October, 1909. Then, after tragically carrying three stillborn boys in a row, another girl, Dan-Yee, was born.

Grandpa Lee was distraught over the fact that he had no son, so Ada, his favorite, was treated almost as a surrogate boy. She was dressed as a boy and shown all the deference a Chinese family in those days usually reserved for a son. From the time she was five or six years old until she was eleven, Grandpa Lee would take young Ada, dressed as a boy, on his regular excursions to the town brothels. Ada would be met by a male household servant at the school yard gate and he would accompany her to a brothel where she met her father. With him and the other patrons, she would eat and pass the time at the banquet table, particularly enjoying the entertainment accompanying the banquet. By eight o'clock, however, young Ada would start to doze off at the table. Then, while her father stayed on at the brothel, she would be carried home, piggyback style, on the servant's back. Her father was indulgent with Ada, allowing her to get away with anything—and she soon developed a very independent spirit.

In the brothel, Grandpa Lee particularly favored a fresh and sassy girl named A-do. Although an herbal tea, which was supposed to be a foolproof form of sterilization, was drunk by all the girls who worked in the brothel, in A-do's case, the tea was not effective. The other girls claimed that she had routinely dumped the tea in the spittoon. In any case, she was soon carrying Grandpa Lee's unborn child. From that point on A-do acted very proud and aloof, knowing that her special circumstance set her apart from the rest of the girls in the brothel. Grandpa Lee, anxious to have a son, soon purchased A-do from the brothel and installed her at his home as his third wife. Her first born was a boy and, following his birth, she produced two more sons in rapid succession. Grandpa Lee, now the father of three boys, was utterly happy—though Ada still held on to her position as the favorite. Shan-dah, the daughter of the first wife and the least favorite, disliked her life at home. After her mother died, she decided to marry at an early age and to accompany her new husband, Chou, to a university in Shanghai where he was studying to be a medical doctor.

When Ada turned fourteen, she began to blossom into a rare beauty. She discarded her boy's clothing and soon developed a life-long passion for fashionable clothes. Her fair complexion was particularly complemented by a special palette of pastel colors— soft peach, turquoise, mint and her favorite, pale lavender. Her father opened unlimited accounts for her at the town's best yardage store and with her favorite dressmaker. She soon became well known in Wusi for her outstanding wardrobe. She was, in today's terms, a "power shopper." Through never-ending exploration and experimentation, she developed a style that was uniquely her own. One day, while shopping, she noticed a local girl wearing a most unusual outfit. The fabric was like nothing she had ever seen before.

The dress was so amazing and exquisite in its details that she boldly inquired as to its source. The girl, who had gone to school in Shanghai for the past year, replied that she acquired most of her wardrobe in that capital of fine fashion. The seed was planted in Ada's mind. She immediately tried to convince her father to let her attend a boarding school in Shanghai. At first he refused to consider the idea on the grounds that she was too young to venture alone to Shanghai, with its reputation throughout China as the "City of Sin." Nevertheless, Ada schemed with her best friend and cousin, Jeh (anglicized later to Jill), and they both applied to and got accepted by an all-girls boarding school in Shanghai. After much haranguing and negotiation, the two willful girls finally obtained their fathers' permission to go to the big city.

In 1924, Ada and her cousin Jill arrived in Shanghai, the most cosmopolitan city in the Far East. Amidst the full swing of the roaring twenties, the city was teeming with European and American jazz babies and flappers. Ada immediately immersed into the fad along with a large group of modern Chinese girls.

In the middle of the first semester, Grandpa Lee paid Ada a visit. In stark contrast to the well-dressed cosmopolitan gentlemen of Shanghai, he looked, with his Chinese robe and cotton shoes, like someone from a feudal society. Ada was so embarrassed that she refused to accompany him to dinner. Instead, she took him back to the train station for his return trip to Wusi—before too many of her friends at the dormitory had a chance to meet him. Only a few years later, when Ada was in her senior year of high school, Grandpa Lee died suddenly of a heart attack. Later in life, she deeply regretted her embarrassment during that visit and, when she spoke of it, always had tears in her eyes.

From her early school years, with her nightly banquets at brothels, Ada never developed good study habits. At the end of her first school year in Shanghai she knew that she would never make it through another year at this particular school. Although Jill was doing fine, Ada convinced her to transfer with her to a fashionable school for party-loving rich kids. The tuition was high but the students could earn passing grades with minimum effort. Ada and Jill got a small apartment in the city together since the school was without boarding facilities. Both girls' parents assumed that the expensive tuition meant that the school provided a quality education. In fact, however, Ada and Jill spent most of their time at the cinema, restaurants and parties.

After Grandpa Lee died, his third wife, A-do, because she was the bearer of his sons, immediately took control of the family finances. With A-do in charge, Ada was concerned about whether or not her mother and her younger sister, Dan-Yee, would be properly provided for. Ada was strong and forceful with A-do, however, and obtained from her a commitment for sufficient funds to cover her own and her sister's education. Adamant that Dan-Yee should receive the best education, Ada immediately brought her to Shanghai and enrolled her at St. Mary's Boarding School, an American Missionary school with exceptionally high educational standards. The faculty were mostly Americans and the curriculum was taught entirely in English. When Dan-Yee first arrived in Shanghai from Wusi, she spoke very little English, but Ada used her connections to find her sister an English tutor. The tutor, Soong, was a law school student who spoke excellent English. He taught Dan-Yee for eighteen months, until he left Shanghai for advanced studies in England. During the time he tutored her, Soong fell in love with Dan-Yee. Two years later, when she was just seventeen years old, he returned from England and they married in a small and simple ceremony with only Ada and Jill attending.

Meanwhile, in Wusi, Ada's mother, Grandma Lee, was quite unhappy. Her meager expenses were doled out by the tight-fisted A-do who constantly made nasty remarks about the "sonless" Grandma Lee. As time went on these nasty remarks escalated into screaming fits. Gentle by nature and traditional throughout, down to her tiny bound feet, Grandma Lee suffered silently, only pouring out her woes in letters to her beloved Ada in Shanghai. Ada soon developed an intense dislike of her father's third wife. She vowed to herself that one day she would show A-do how much better her stepdaughter was than any of her sons.

Chapter Five

After finishing high school, Ada entered college, enrolling in a prelaw program. She transferred to physical education, however, after only one semester. She was having a hard time with every college program she chose, in part because, during this time, her dating increased from occasional to constant. She was busy evaluating each beau's potential as a future husband, conscious of the pressing need to somehow free her mother from A-do's household.

Through her circle of friends, she met a young physician and his pretty wife, Dr. and Mrs. King. Dr. King, an OB-GYN, wanted to build his own private hospital. To obtain the financing, he announced that the new hospital would have a special department serving needy pregnant women who couldn't afford medical care on their own. A massive fund-raising campaign was launched for this good cause, and Ada, who knew many well-to-do people, threw herself wholeheartedly into the campaign. She mobilized all her friends to contribute and help raise funds for this charity. Before long, the goal was met, with Ada personally raising enough money to equip the entire operating room. Dr. King secured a bank loan for the balance needed and his dream became a reality. A four-story red-brick building, adjoined by manicured grounds, was constructed on one of Shanghai's most fashionable avenues. It was equipped with American and European medical supplies and equipment and had the most advanced operating room in all of China. Dr. King named it "China Convalescent Hospital." The only resident physician, Dr. King was in charge of the free services to needy expectant mothers. This program, however, only represented a small portion of the hospital's business. Primarily, it catered to very rich patients. The accommodations had more of a resort hotel atmosphere than that of a traditional hospital, and wealthy people would check in for each little sneeze or cough. Patients were required to bring with them their own personal physicians, and the hospital provided a first-rate nursing staff to take care of their every wish.

Dr. and Mrs. King took the entire fourth floor of the building eight thousand square feet—as their personal residence, a large and comfortable arrangement by anyone's standards. To show their gratitude to Ada for her fund raising effort, Dr. and Mrs. King offered Ada and Jill accommodations at their residence. Dr. King planned to teach a class at the hospital to train midwives and, since he knew Ada's continuing problem with school, he guaranteed her graduation from this two-year course. Ada and Jill readily took him up on the offer and moved into Dr. King's China Convalescent Hospital in the fall of 1928. During the two year course, however, Ada and Jill seldom attended any classes.

Jill, who had a bad case of acne and was slightly overweight, usually stayed home every night dateless. Ada, on the other hand, was never home any evening unless she was seriously ill. She dated a series of fashionable young men, many of whom rubbed elbows with the British residents of Shanghai. They drove their own automobiles and were members of the prestigious Country Club or Jockey Club. They spent their daytime hours at the race track, the Greyhound track or the jai alai fonton—a popular gambling pastime in Shanghai at that time, Nights were spent dining and dancing at the city's numerous night clubs. The popular Ada had acquired an astonishing wardrobe for both day and evening. Her evening attire always consisted of a formal gown, which combined the fashion of east and west—high collared mandarin-style tops with sleeves and long flowing skirts which showed well on the dance floor. Ada also earned a reputation as the most accomplished ballroom dancer in her circle.

At her two-year midwife course, however, Ada accomplished very little. Due to her aversion to blood, she never watched an actual delivery of a baby. At the strategic time she usually ran to a restaurant down the street and drowned her nausea with an ice cream soda. Despite Ada's shortcomings, she and Jill became very close friends with Mrs. King. At the end of two years, she offered them both lifetime employment at the hospital. Jill took a job as the official greeter/receptionist, but Ada was not interested in something which would tie her down all day long. Instead, she managed to become Dr. King's "assistant." His routine was to make a personal visit to all the patients at ten a.m., finishing around noontime. This suited Ada perfectly. She would spend less than two hours a day wearing a white coat and following Dr. King on his rounds. The balance of the day was then available for shopping and tea dances, before her nightly routine of dating, dinner and dancing.

The charity department for pregnant mothers had provided patients for the midwife classes. Now that the first midwife course was over, Dr. King decided to abolish both the charity department and the school. The hospital had become a great success in the first two years and he wanted to use the space for profit-making purposes. Ada, though upset that the good cause for which she had raised funds was going to be abolished, could not say much about Dr. King's decision. He was now her employer, and she collected a full salary plus free accommodations for only two hours of work a day.

One day, while doing his rounds in the hospital, Dr. King took particular notice of a woman patient, and a love affair soon developed. This very wealthy woman became a regular patient in the hospital, even though there was nothing wrong with her. It wasn't long before Dr. King's marriage was on the verge of breaking up. Frequent arguments and fights upset the usual tranquillity of the apartment above the hospital. Ada knew that if Dr. King divorced his wife, she and Jill would both lose their setup in the hospital. Jill could return back home to Wusi, but this was not an option for Ada. With her work and living arrangement in jeopardy,

Frank J. Leo

she had to move into high gear in her effort to find a husband. Among her many suitors, there were three for whom she had a special feeling. The first was a playboy who lived on an allowance from his very strict father. He had not done well in school and didn't possess any particular skills for making a living. The second was ordered by his parents to return home to marry a woman, with bound feet, whom he had never met. He felt he had to obey, but immediately after the wedding ceremony caught a train back to Shanghai and the marriage was never consummated. As long as his mother was living, however, he wouldn't divorce this wife. To make matters worse, his father had stopped his allowance in hopes of forcing him back home. Neither of these two suitors was remotely what Ada was looking for in a husband.

The third suitor, however, was tall and handsome, always meticulously dressed, fluent in English, and well educated with a background in law. He was doing quite well financially and was caring for his widowed mother. His name was Frank Woo. Ada began to date him exclusively for several months and soon fell in love with him. One night he was supposed to pick her up for an evening of dinner and dancing, but he never came, nor did he call. In the weeks and months which followed, he just disappeared from the face of the earth without a trace. Ada was devastated.

Brokenhearted, she took refuge at the home of her aunt. This aunt's husband turned out to be a relative of Zee's. One day Zee, while in Shanghai to visit the couple, met Ada for the first time. At that very first meeting, Zee decided that this woman was to be his wife. He repeatedly proposed to Ada during the week both of them were house guests, but she turned him down each time. Ada didn't think Zee was for her. Obviously an old-fashioned man from a small town, he was not cosmopolitan like the men she had been dating—other cities were considered hokey small towns by most Shanghai residents. On the other hand, Ada did think Zee was tall and not too bad looking. Ada's aunt decided to do a little matchmaking. She made a list of Zee's strong points as a potential husband. At the top of the list was the immense wealth of Zee's family—none of Ada's other suitors could even come close. With his father at a very advanced age, he would take control of the family fortune in no time. Aside from his family wealth, Ada's aunt listed Zee's good points as gentle, kind and best of all, generous. Ada, however, still wasn't convinced. Knowing that her mother's security was foremost on Ada's mind, her aunt told Zee of Ada's mother's predicament. Zee laughed and said that her mother would be treated like his own mother in the family compound, and would be waited on by dozens of servants around the clock. He instructed Ada's aunt to inform her that if she agreed to marry him, he would give her everything under the sun and, to make her happy, would do anything her heart desired. Given the uncertainty of her and her mother's future, Zee started to look better to Ada as the days went on. But she was still hesitant. Though he seemed to be good husband material, in her heart she knew she was not in love with this man who seemed to adore her. In addition, she was concerned about Zee's parents. She wondered how they would react to Zee's wild promises to her, as well as to having a modern woman like herself as a potential daughter-in-law. In an effort to put her concerns to rest, Zee suggested a meeting with his parents.

Ada agreed to this meeting and gave serious thought as to how she should present herself. She decided that honesty would be best. She wanted them to accept her as she was—a modern Shanghai girl. Knowing that Zee's parents were older, very traditional and conservative, she deliberately chose a fashionable figure-flattering ensemble. She wore a lavender silk Chinese dress with matching high heels. Over her shoulder she draped a white wool coat and topped off the outfit with an outlandish white angora French beret. Zee arranged the meeting with Ada and his parents at his parents' hotel suite in Shanghai.

Grandma was extremely enthusiastic upon first seeing Ada. To her delight, Ada was beautiful beyond her greatest expectations, surpassing even the glowing and detailed reports of their son. Ada's best feature was her luminous creamy white and absolutely flawless skin—her complexion was described by her friends as a shelled hard-boiled egg. Her eyes were her second most commanding feature. They were almond in shape and unusually bright, with a sparkle that came from within. She was petite, five-feet tall, and weighed less than one hundred pounds. She looked extra delicate next to Grandpa, Grandma, and a strapping six-foot tall Zee. Ada lit a cigarette as soon as she sat down, part of her well prepared presentation. Subconsciously, perhaps, she was hoping that Zee's parents would reject her and relieve her from this difficult decision. Grandma, however, immediately positioned herself next to Ada on a settee, grasped her hands and animatedly engaged her in conversation. She took an immediate liking to Ada. Ada was not at all prepared when Grandma threw her arms around her in a both figurative and real embrace. She nearly tipped over the ash tray holding her cigarette but soon realized that Zee's mother had a genuine fondness of her, and a real rapport began to develop between them.

Grandpa was also enthusiastic when he first saw Ada. He thought that his seemingly useless son had, at least on this occasion, made an excellent choice. This auspicious meeting marked the first time in the family history that a marriage was planned by choice on the part of the bride and groom-to-be. Since Ada was an independent young woman, it was not necessary to obtain the consent of any member of her family. Grandma, however, detected a reluctance in Ada and took an aggressive stance, not wanting to let this girl hesitate and slip away. Ada finally succumbed and agreed to marry Zee. Overnight, a lavish engagement party was arranged. Zee purchased for Ada a beautiful engagement ring, carved out of a solid piece of apple green Burmese jade.

The engagement ceremony was almost as formal as an actual wedding, complete with a grand banquet. It was attended by over two hundred guests. Ada's friends came mostly from Shanghai, and Zee's retinue primarily from Changchow. The guests from Changchow were more than willing to take the three-hour train ride to witness their infamous local son get engaged to a modern social butterfly in Shanghai. Zee's parents were so elated that their son was finally settling down to wedded bliss that the cost of the party was of no consequence. Zee himself was on "cloud nine." Ada was swept up into this elation as well, thinking that this might be the right decision after all.

Chapter Six ———————————————————

After the ceremony, Grandpa and Grandma returned home to their country estate in a jubilant mood. Grandma examined, cleaned and stowed all her good jewelry in a large locked chest, wearing the key on a gold chain around her neck. She looked forward to giving the key to the new bride on their wedding day. As fate would have it, however, a few months after the engagement, Grandma had a severe heart attack and expired within hours. Only weeks before, she had celebrated her forty-sixth birthday. In a time when monitoring blood pressure and related preventive measures were not customary, her many years of being overweight surely contributed to her demise. When the pain gripped her heart, her last thought was her treasure chest with her vast collection of heirloom and contemporary jewelry. In the spaces between the jewelry boxes, she had also jammed hundreds of gold bars weighing approximately ten taels (a unit of weight heavier than an ounce) each. She clutched the key around her neck as she collapsed to the floor and, after she died, it took a couple of people to pry the key from her hand. Years later, the key was given to Ada. By then, however, all that was left in it were a couple of handfuls of loose pearls. In a large family, it was very easy for valuables to vanish forever.

In the tradition of the times, Ada's and Zee's wedding was postponed until after the required three-year mourning period following the death of a parent. Zee was naturally very unhappy about both his mother's death and the long postponement of his marriage. During the three-year period, he made regular monthly visits to Shanghai to see Ada, who was still living in the hospital apartment. Ada, meanwhile, was beginning to vacillate about her impending wedding. She also didn't allow her engagement to slow down her social activities and, when Zee came to call, frequently asked Jill to entertain him while she was out at parties. Zee never complained. He often spent an evening at the apartment dining and chatting with Jill until the wee hours, when Ada would eventually return from her outing. In Ada's opinion, Zee, in his traditional Chinese robes, was just not suave enough to accompany her to Shanghai social functions. After her return from an evening out, she would usually spend only fifteen minutes with Zee and then send him on to his hotel—she needed her sleep. As this went on month after month, Zee's patience and easygoing temperament started to make Ada feel guilty.

One night, she walked into the apartment in stocking feet with her satin dance pumps in her hands and found Zee and Jill enjoying a late night game of chess. She realized that the time had come for a talk. Jill retired to her room to give them privacy, and Zee feared the worst. Feeling that she was going to back out of the engagement, he quickly assured her that she should never feel guilty about going out. His first concern was her happiness. If it made her happy to go out dancing, she should do it without reservations. Ada was touched. Finally, however, she mustered enough strength to utter in a low voice, "I'm not the right girl for you. Look at Jill! She has everything I don't have. She is very bright, and you get along so well with her. She could make you a wonderful wife."

"Ada! You are the only girl for me," Zee insisted.

Ada explained that her world was a social one. From the moment she arrived in Shanghai as a teenager, she had enjoyed this life. She was sure she was not the kind of wife Zee would want. Zee responded, pleading,

"Ada! As long as you are happy, it is all right with me. As you know, my father is getting on in years. One day I will be handling the family finances. I can give you any kind of life you want. I could buy you a house in Shanghai. You could come to Shanghai as often as you want and keep all your Shanghai friends and social activities."

Ada realized she had lost her argument when Zee added, "You must realize that no one else could give your mother a better life than I could."

With this conversation, Ada gave up the idea of canceling her engagement. After that, the time passed quickly. Zee had overcome his drug dependency and was working energetically, planning and overseeing the construction of a large new addition to the ancestral home for the newlyweds' quarters. Every modern convenience was included, even up-to-date western-style plumbing, the first such installation in the compound. Electricity had been in use throughout the homestead for a few years, but the lighting was much more refined in the new wing. The sumptuous bridal suite was the talk of the town. At the close of the official mourning period, the final construction details were completed, and everyone awaited the arrival of the new young bride.

Chapter Seven ─────────

The wedding was to be held in a Shanghai hotel of Ada's choice. Dozens of railroad cars were chartered to transport the guests of the groom from Changchow and the bride's guests from Wusi. Hundreds of hotel rooms were booked to accommodate the out-of-town guests. Since Ada's father had passed away, the Minister of Finance in Chiang Kai-Shek's government, who had married a former handmaiden at the Liu family compound, was asked to give the bride away.

The wedding party was attired in a mix of Western and Chinese style clothing. Ada chose a western-style gown made from cream toned silk peau de soie with double cape sleeves. She wore matching opera-length gloves and a cap of Aleceon lace with a cathedral length veil of English net, embroidered with chrysanthemums. The groom wore western-style white tie and tails. Grandfather wore traditional brocaded Chinese formal attire. The young boys serving as train bearer and ring bearer were attired in the formal style of the English court, much like Little Lord Fauntleroy. The flower girl wore a red velvet Chinese-style dress trimmed with ermine. The bride was hailed as a fashion pioneer in 1934 Shanghai where western style weddings were rarely seen. The ceremony itself, however, was still in the Chinese tradition.

The bride and the groom bowed to all four witnesses individually, then bowed to each other. Afterwards, they each stamped the wedding certificate with their personal chops or seals. The ceremony was followed by a formal portrait sitting. The photographer, an Englishman, differed with Grandpa Liu's opinion that, since he was elder, he should be seated and the bride should be standing. The Englishman won out and in the final portrait the bride was allowed to sit beside her father-in-law.

After the photo session, Ada retired to the hotel's bridal suite to change. She removed the western style gown and accessories. A hairdresser pulled her permanent waved hair into a tight chignon and added several hair pieces to create the look of a traditional aristocratic Chinese lady. Dozens of pearls were woven through her hair. On the right side above her forehead, a phoenix bird made from pearls was woven on golden wire. In the bird's beak, a cascade of strands of seed pearls dangled in front of her right eye. On her ears, she wore large cluster earrings, with pearls falling from them as well. She donned a traditional ensemble—a floor length skirt and a form fitting jacket with Mandarin collar, all made from soft red satin and red satin Chinese slippers. The entire outfit was elaborately embroidered with blooming peonies and song birds. Zee changed into a traditional robe of deep blue matte satin with a black matte silk Mandarin Jacket.

After the changeover, Ada and Zee returned to the more than five hundred guests in the ballroom for the Chinese part of the ceremony, a formalized introduction of the families. Grandfather and Mrs. Upstairs, his only remaining wife, were seated in the center and first received the kneeling courtesy of the bride and groom. Then, Grandma Lee was given the same respectful bow. Following that, hundreds of cousins from both sides of the family were broken down into small groups to be introduced to the newlyweds. They all bowed formally. Then, the new couple were seated to receive the numerous nieces and nephews, who knelt before them. This presentation ceremony lasted several hours, and was immediately followed by the banquet. The guests were seated at round tables of ten and the newlyweds were obligated to present themselves at each table to drink a toast. The bride and groom were wise enough to barely allow their lips to touch the toasting goblets. The feast lasted until the early hours of the morning.

The newlyweds recovered from the elaborate ceremony, resting for two days at their hotel before departing for Changchow. Ada had never been to that part of China before and had only heard stories about the place that was to be her home. In her heart, she was still not sure that she had done the right thing. Nevertheless, everything was set and westward she traveled to a new home and a new life.

Chapter Eight ────────────────

Ada's marriage did not come one minute too soon. By the time she married, Dr. and Mrs. King were divorced and he had married the woman patient with whom he had fallen in love. The first Mrs. King had left China for Germany to study medicine, later returning to Shanghai and becoming a very successful pediatrician in Shanghai. Soon after the new Mrs. King moved into the penthouse above the hospital, Dr. King announced that both Ada and Jill had to find employment and accommodations elsewhere. Since Ada's wedding was only a few weeks away, he allowed them to stay until Ada moved with her new husband to Changchow. Jill then returned to her parents' home in Wusi, but the two women still maintained their close friendship.

Two days after her wedding, Ada, Zee and the family embarked on the three-hour train trip to Changchow. When they arrived at the train station in Changchow, hundreds of onlookers were waiting on the platform, eager to get a glimpse of the new bride from Shanghai. Four large sedan chairs, each carried by eight men, were outside the station, ready to transport the wedding party to the compound. Each chair was like a small room, complete with roof and side curtains. The first three were for Grandfather, Mrs. Upstairs and Ada's mother, Mrs. Lee. The fourth one, completely decorated with embroidered red satin, was for the bride, the "New Madam" as she would be called by everyone at the Changchow compound. Zee rode a white horse behind Ada's sedan chair. The rest of the entourage followed in a long line of rickshaws. The compound was bright and shining in anticipation of the arrival of the newlyweds, the ten sets of heavy red lacquered double gates wide open in a straight line. Everyone got off their rickshaws at the front gate and Zee dismounted his horse. The four sedan chairs, however, were carried through all the courtyards to the last main hall. To Ada, the last set of gates looked miles away in the distance. Awed by the pageantry and tradition, she knew she was beginning a very different life from the one she had led in Shanghai.

To show respect to her new in-laws, Ada tried to be a perfect wife and ideal daughter-in-law. She was careful to carry herself in a dignified manner, and to follow the customs of this very traditional household. She rose each morning by seven thirty. After she dressed and did her make up, the first item of the day was a short but polite visit to her last remaining mother-in-law, Mrs. Upstairs. Then, promptly at nine-thirty, she arrived for breakfast with her new father-in-law. Zee and his brother, Chi, went horseback riding every morning at six. After their ride in the country, they would bathe and return to bed, so Ada usually had breakfast alone with her father-in-law. They sat at breakfast in silence on large uncomfortable straight back dining room chairs. The back of the chair was too far for Ada to lean against. In addition, a maid would have to bring her a foot stool since Ada's feet did not reach the floor. Unlike during their first meeting, she never lit a cigarette in Grandfather's presence, because he did not smoke. She also showed respect to her father-in-law by not speaking unless she was addressed first, and staying seated until Grandfather rose from the table. Since he was already in his eighties, he ate very slowly and seldom spoke, so this silent breakfast would often last almost until lunch time. Ada felt imprisoned by the daily morning ritual but she didn't shirk from what she considered her duty. Sometimes there would be only a ten to fifteen minute break between breakfast and lunch, and then the same ritual would start all over again.

During the break, Ada would race to the bridal apartment and try to encourage her husband to accompany her to lunch, which was always served promptly at noon. Although Zee had cleaned up his opium addiction before the wedding, he still had the habit of spending a good deal of the daylight hours in bed. Ada knew that her father-in-law disapproved of Zee's lazy habits, and she felt it was her responsibility to get Zee to appear at the daily lunch table. During the first month of their marriage, she even got him to show up at the breakfast table. The first time Ada dined with Grandfather at the compound, she chose a seat across from the old man at the square table. Grandfather quickly addressed one of the nearby servants, "Please seat the New Madam to my side." Afterwards, Ada found out from Zee that the seat across from him was reserved for his sons. If anyone else took that seat it was considered disrespectful. Ada wondered why Grandfather had not addressed her directly instead of asking the servant to move her elsewhere. Zee laughed at her bewilderment, "You are a merchant's daughter who is now living in an aristocratic home. It will take you years to learn all of our customs, but don't worry, father is too old to remember all your faux pas."

Zee arrived for meals later and later as time went by, finally only appearing at dinner time. Fortunately for Ada, the lunches did not drag on endlessly. Grandfather routinely retired to his study for an afternoon nap, and Ada was free to accept the invitations of various relatives in the compound to spend the afternoon playing Mahjong and having tea. She learned to enjoy the game and, as time passed, became an expert. Very often, in the middle of a game, a servant would run in and announce that the Old Master was leaving his study and heading for the dining room. Ada would have to drop everything and rush back to the dinner table—on time.

Life at the compound followed time-honored traditions as part of everyday life and during every holiday as well. Ada had arrived at her new home in the fall, only a short time before the year's biggest celebration, the Chinese New Year. On New Year's eve, according to tradition, the shrine was opened and, every year, Miss Vegetarian took extraordinary steps to prepare for this most important event. Ada was awed by the large-scale display of pageantry which took place. As Grandfather led the way, family members lined up single file and each one knelt at the central table, paying their respect to the ancestors. The shrine was unheated and wide open, and everyone braved the icy night air wearing their formal robes lined with sable or wild mink. The silent procession was attended by over a hundred family members. Ada was gradually being inducted into a world of tradition that she had never before imagined. She had no idea then that it would soon be gone forever.

Chapter Nine ─────────────

The large compound was like a village unto itself. There were over a hundred servants and their families who lived on the premises, and it was not uncommon to see scores of children running about. Ada was always meeting new people, but everyone, of course, already knew who she was. Though at times it was difficult to remember all the new faces, Ada soon became familiar with most.

One day, a little girl about four or five years old, ran past Ada. As soon as the child saw her, like everyone else, she stopped and greeted the New Madam. Ada smiled, returned the greeting and thought nothing more of the encounter. As the days passed, Ada saw the girl a few more times. She noticed that the child was always in the company of a woman servant, yet the servant did not seem to be the child's mother. One day Ada asked the woman who the child was. The woman swept the child into her arms in a wave of nervous giggles and disappeared through a doorway. Needless to say, that piqued Ada's curiosity. Ada had also noticed certain facial resemblance between the child and her new husband. Among all the servants, the breakfast cook, a woman in her sixties, had the longest tenure of service, so Ada figured she would be a good reliable source of information. The cook hurried into Ada's quarters, hearing that the New Madam wished to see her, and Ada asked about this little girl. The cook knew that the truth could no longer be hidden. She revealed the little girl's background to Ada. The child was the daughter of a former handmaiden in Zee's mother's household, and Zee was the father. The mother was married off years ago, and the baby had been raised and pampered by Zee's mother and her servants. Since the death of Zee's mother, she was left in the care of a nanny and had gotten kind of "lost in the shuffle." Ada felt sorry for the little girl but was furious with Zee for covering up this story. She didn't want to show any outward anger, however, fearing that Grandfather would disapprove of a daughter-in-law with a bad temperament. So, she had a quiet discussion with Zee in the privacy of their bedroom. She expressed her anger about Zee's not telling the truth, even though this happened before they met. At this early stage of their marriage she already felt deceived and wronged. Zee pleaded and begged for her forgiveness. He said that he was afraid she would have refused to marry him had she known of his tarnished past. He also promised that there would be no wish of hers which he would not fulfill if she would forgive him this one thing. Ada said that she would remind him of his promise in the future.

Ada decided to raise the child as her own daughter and moved Ivy and her nanny into her quarters, insisting that the child address her as "Mommie," instead of New Madam. Unbeknownst to Ada, her name had often been used by the servants in disciplining the little girl. Ivy had regularly been told that the New Madam would not be pleased if she misbehaved. She had naturally developed a dislike for and fear of this New Madam, even before she met Ada. In the beginning, therefore, their relationship was a little strained.

Although Ada's social activities while living on the compound were not at all like those during her life in Shanghai, she learned to enjoy a new activity, the Peking Opera. The Liu family was considered "patron of the arts," including, of course, the Peking Opera. The classical opera companies all stopped in Changchow during their tours and the stars of the various companies would visit major patrons in person, including Grandfather, prior to their opening performances. In addition to making a generous contribution, Grandfather also bought a block of the best seats for every performance through the duration of the booking. The tickets were available for anyone in the compound who was interested in attending. This was Ada's first exposure to the Peking Opera and she soon became an avid fan. The regular performances, the easy availability of tickets and perhaps the need to step outside of the compound prompted her to attend again and again.

Another new experience for Ada was becoming accustomed to the rich food which was served at the daily meals. The breakfast, prepared in a separate kitchen by the breakfast cook, always included a rice porridge, plus many varieties of dim-sum. Lunch and dinner consisted of an array of meats and vegetables elaborately prepared by the chef in the main kitchen. Plenty of pork lard was used in the many stir-fry dishes, and the various sauces were all extra heavy and rich. After a while, Ada grew tired of the endless selection of banquet style dishes and requested a plate of vegetables and tofu, simply prepared with very little oil in a mild sauce. This brought gales of laughter from all the servants, who gossiped about how the New Madam favored peasant food. Soon, Ada's aversion to rich food intensified so much that she felt nauseous from the mere odor of the dishes. Everyone realized then that the New Madam was with child.

In the early stages of her pregnancy, Ada still maintained her morning routine at the breakfast table. But, as time passed, it became more and more difficult for her to sit for hours in the straight-backed teak dining room chair. Finally, Grandfather took notice of her discomfort. He instructed the servants to provide a lounge chair for the New Madam after she finished eating. This small bit of comfort was little relief, however, because she was still obligated to remain in the dining room until Grandfather left. Her craving for tobacco heightened also, and she looked forward to visits from other members of the compound in the late morning so she could sneak a puff from their cigarettes when Grandfather was distracted.

Midway through Ada's pregnancy, Jill came to visit. To Ada's delight, Jill planned to stay until after the birth. During Ada's years in Changchow, Jill spent at least four or five months of the year as a house guest of the estate. She was well liked by Grandfather and was addressed as "Miss Jill" by everyone in the compound. Zee's two sisters, Miss No. 1 and Miss No. 2, also arrived for their annual four-months' long vacation, each now with a four-year old boy in tow. Ada welcomed the chance to have extra people at the daily meals. As her time drew near, Ada felt that it would be best for her child to be delivered in a Shanghai hospital, but Zee convinced her that, in order to put to rest the rumors that filled the air, Grandfather's idea of having the baby at home, with many eye witnesses, would be the best.

Chapter Ten

T he most important event to take place, prior to my birth itself, was the selection of a wet nurse. In those days, according to custom, an upper class Chinese lady would never breast-feed her baby for fear that her breasts would increase in size—and women with large breasts were definitely considered lower class. A wet nurse, usually a peasant woman who had a baby at approximately the same time as the society lady, would be hired to nurse the baby. A woman with several children generally could not find anyone to care for all of her children and thus could not work as a wet nurse. New mothers with their first child, however, could put their baby in the care of another village woman and go to the city to nurse other women's babies. Many young married couples needed this supplementary income to get started in life. A wet nurse hired by a wealthy family usually received a very high salary, as well as a good diet and medical care. By working in that position for eight months to a year, a young mother could put aside quite a bit of cash to take home after her services were no longer required.

Before I was born, there were many applicants for the wet nurse position. The most important criteria in the selection of a wet nurse was the richness of her milk. To determine this, the applicant was asked to squirt some of her milk onto a piece of highly polished teak wood. If the milk beaded up, it meant it was rich. If the milk ran, however, it was considered too thin and therefore not suitable. Also, the quantity of milk was taken into consideration. If only a few drops could be squeezed out onto the wood, the applicant was quickly rejected. In addition, during that time Chinese families believed that the child would take on a thirty-percent likeness of the breast milk provider. Therefore, Ada insisted on a good-looking wet nurse. Also, with Ada's experience in the medical field, my wet nurse was the first one on the compound to have a blood test to check for venereal diseases. This was done at the family hospital, adjoining the compound. After considering many applicants, Ada finally chose a wet nurse. She was tall by Chinese standards, with big eyes, a straight nose and a slight Caucasian look which pleased Ada. She came to work the day I was born. Since she was nursing the most important person in the household, she was treated like a queen by everyone. Ada made sure that no one said a harsh word to this woman, including Zee and her brother-in-law, Chi. Ada feared that if the wet nurse got upset, her milk might turn sour. The wet nurse quickly learned the pecking order in the household and was soon the queen of all the hired help. Even the masters and mistresses in the compound had to speak to her in gentle and polite tones. Displaying a grandiose attitude because of her lofty position, she was very demanding with her daily meals, often pointed out mistakes to the staff and made other servants run errands and fulfill her every wish.

Her reign did not last very long, however. After just a few months, her milk mysteriously ran dry. She was afraid to lose her golden position, so she didn't tell anyone about her dried-up breasts. When no one was watching, she would feed me some rice soup. Soon, I was ill from malnutrition. I ran a high temperature and my tongue was covered with blisters. Ada was in a state of panic. The doctors were baffled, because malnutrition is difficult to detect in the early stages. One afternoon, as my gravely distraught mother sat in my nursery, I started to fuss and the wet nurse began to nurse me. After a few minutes, I fussed again, so the wet nurse switched me to the other nipple in an effort to quiet me. Suspicious, Ada inquired, "How's your milk lately?"

"I've been a little low on milk the last couple of days," answered the wet nurse, smiling sheepishly.

Ada jumped out of her chair. She called in several servant women and asked them to bring the all-telling polished teak plaque. Try as she might, the wet nurse could not squeeze out a single drop of milk onto the wood. None at all! Ada charged out of the room, furious. This was such a major family disaster. Zee came in and started to yell at the wet nurse, who was by now sobbing loudly. The most important matter, however, was to find a new wet nurse immediately. Everyone in the compound was mobilized into action for this emergency. In a matter of hours, a new qualified wet nurse was located, but her gaping hare lip stopped Ada in her tracks. The thirty percent likeness was taken very seriously indeed. Considering the starving baby, however, Ada promised the hare-lipped woman a huge sum of cash to feed the baby for just two days. She was certain that a suitable wet nurse could be found in that period of time. In the meantime, a large silk folding fan, with the painting of an imperial court beauty, was held by a maid to cover the wet nurse's face every time she breast fed me.

Two day's later, a perfect wet nurse was found. She was a young mother, barely twenty, a petite but healthy girl, and unusually attractive. I became healthy again quickly, but everyone said that my thin long neck was due to that period of starvation.

The original wet nurse, in a state of tears and torment, lamented that she was very poor and that her husband was counting on her earnings for the year. She had hidden the truth because she knew that she would lose her employment and her income. After her rage subsided, the soft-hearted Ada felt sorry for this woman. She agreed to keep her as a servant for the year at her wet nurse's salary. But, her queenly status at the compound quickly vanished.

No matter how attractive my wet nurses, I was still far from being a pretty baby. My head, large in proportion to my body, was connected by a skinny long neck, and always looked precariously in danger of snapping off. With a few brownish hairs on top, this elongated head of mine sported a huge protruding forehead and back skull, unlike the round flat heads covered with thick black hair of most Chinese babies. Looking at me from the front, my forehead seemed to take up half of my face.

I was odd looking for sure, but I was still the world's most perfect jewel in my Grandfather's eyes. He came to the nursery every day to hold me in his arms. He was so fragile that he was only allowed to hold me if his maids, the wet nurse, as well as Ada, formed a group surrounding him and me. Grandfather would regale me with a barrage of baby talk, as though he and I were alone together. He cooed about my unusual head, saying that I had a pot of gold in the front and a pot of silver in the back. He also repeatedly insisted that I was actually the reincarnation of a Buddha or a saintly person. His affection was demonstrated so openly and frequently that everyone was aware of his immense love for his new grandson. Soon, however, his health took a turn for the worse and his visits to the nursery became less frequent. When I was only nine months old, he passed away. His funeral was very elaborate, with mourners from all over China and all walks of life attending. As he had wished, he was buried in a heavenly setting on his beloved Horseshoe Island in Taiwu Lake.

Chapter Eleven _____

After Grandfather passed away, my father became a different person. He no longer spent the days resting or in recreational pursuits, but completely immersed himself in the business world, taking over Grandfather's businesses and working at them from dawn until dusk. He was soon able to maintain the high level of profit in Grandfather's business holdings, and some even yielded more than before. With the large family cash reserves, he decided to build a luxurious villa on Horseshoe Island, large enough to accommodate his family, his brother and his two sisters' families. He did continue his daily two-hour horseback ride in the early mornings, but he didn't go back to bed again like he used to.

Uncle Chi was just out of college and he didn't have the slightest interest in the family finances. His time was mostly taken up with girls and basketball. Chi particularly liked the city girls in Shanghai, so he made two or three trips a month to that glamorous city. He also maneuvered to get a sizable allowance from his older brother, much more than Grandfather had been willing to dole out.

Ada also found a new sense of freedom after grandfather's death. For the first time since she married, she could set her own hours. Mrs. Upstairs, always diplomatic, casually suggested that

Ada's daily visit should be changed to early afternoon due to her meditation schedule. This suited Ada perfectly, who loved to sleep late each morning, especially during the winter months. When the weather turned chilly, she would rise when Zee came home for lunch each day. After lunch, Zee went back to work and she would start her elaborate make-up and dressing routine, which usually took two hours. Then, after a quick visit to Mrs. Upstairs' quarters, she would head off to play Mahjong with the ladies of the compound. At eight p.m., she would then dine with Zee, after he finished his day's work. Many evenings after dinner, she went to the theater. If nothing of interest was being offered at the theater, the Mahjong table would beckon again. On some days she might have a session with a music instructor she hired to teach her to sing Peking Operas. Around midnight, Ada and Zee would have a snack—usually rice porridge with red dates, simmered white fungus in sweet syrup, and/or lotus seed broth. Finally, bedtime came after one a.m.

Now that Ada's husband was the man in control of the family fortune, Ada decided to discuss with him a matter which had been preoccupying her since her father died. Ada still had a score to settle with A-do, her father's third wife. Not long after Grandpa Lee's death, A-do had developed a dependence on opium. In a downward spiral visible to all, the Lee family's wealth earned over several generations was quickly depleted. A-do's temper tantrums and her sarcasm about women without sons had also caused years of agony for Ada's mother. Ada felt she was now ready to show A-do, as well as the world, that her stepdaughter was better than any son could ever be. Her plan was greeted with enthusiastic support by Zee, so with the energy and dedication of an athlete in training, Ada hurled herself into her project.

It was a Chinese custom for surviving family members to celebrate the birthday of a revered deceased relative. Ada picked her father's birthday as the occasion to put on a grand show for the benefit of her stepmother A-do. She chose a well-known Buddhist temple in her father's hometown, Wusi, as the site of the celebration and notified A-do of the upcoming event. She invited over a hundred guests from different cities and booked the travel arrangements and accommodations for her guests.

Ada next planned her wardrobe for the occasion. She told Zee that she needed to have a sable coat to wear when she stepped off the train on her return trip to her hometown. Zee told her that there were trunks full of sables in the fur storage. All she needed to do was to call in a furrier to fashion a coat to her liking. For the first time since she moved into the compound, Ada entered one of the storehouses. In a mammoth room, row upon row of cedar chests, stacked to the rafters, were filled with furs of all kinds. What a treasure trove! Several male servants opened and sorted through the chests marked "sables" to show the New Madam the contents. Out came heavy silk embroidered court robes from the classical period, lined with sable. Ada was amazed at the pristine condition of these robes, as well as the sheer size of the garments. What giants Zee's forefathers must have been! Ada realized the value of these antique robes and felt that too much of a garment would be wasted if she tore it apart to fashion a coat for herself. Instead, she purchased a sable coat in Shanghai on one of her monthly shopping trips.

Finally the time came for the journey to her childhood home of Wusi—the sweet moment of revenge. The Liu family rode in a private railroad car on a chartered train. As planned, A-do was at the railroad station to meet Ada. There were many relatives, friends and old neighbors there, too, who remembered Ada as the pretty young girl who had gone off to Shanghai and married one of the richest men in China. A large crowd waited, curious to see the hometown beauty whom they had not seen since she was fifteen years old. Ada did not disappoint them. Her Chinese dress was pale green silk, trimmed with deeper green satin welt. On her shoulders, she draped the new deep brown full-length sable coat. Behind her as she alighted from the train, the wet nurse carried me. I wore an English outfit made of white wool knit with a matching cap, topped with a pompom. Next came Ada's mother, decked out in a beautiful ensemble, flanked by my towering father and even taller Uncle Chi. As the party stepped onto the platform, the crowd uttered an audible "AH-H-H!" As Ada scanned the crowd that day, her always bright eyes were just a bit brighter. When she spotted her stepmother, she hesitated slightly, then approached her with a warm and spontaneous greeting for the crowd to witness.

This was her moment of triumph. A-do greeted Ada and her entourage with her best smile. She giggled loudly and, for everyone to hear, spoke about how "our" Miss Ada had finally come home— and what an honorable daughter for the Lee family she was.

Ada accepted A-do's invitation to stay at the big house where Ada was born and raised. Although a good part of the family fortune had been squandered away, the house was still there, big and impressive, with a western style circular staircase. A-do's three sons were teenagers then. They all laughed at my odd looking head. A-do paid extra special attention to my father and my uncle, calling them First Master and Second Master. In the spirit of hospitality, she also laid out her opium tray to entertain my father and my uncle, and they both enjoyed it immensely. The memorial service, held with great pageantry and dignity, lasted three days. Before our departure, A-do took Zee aside and asked him for some money. Always benevolent, he gave her a sizable check. Little did he or Ada suspect then that this would be the first of many large sums which A-do or her sons would extract from Zee.

Chapter Twelve

When I was fourteen months old, my wet nurse's husband came from the village to fetch his wife. They were a very young couple, and he missed her very much. My wet nurse had a genuine love for me, but she also missed her husband and her own child. Many tears were shed as she bid farewell to all the people she had grown close to in the past year. But fortunately, she would stay in touch with my family throughout my childhood and often visit, even after we moved to Shanghai. She would bring a gift from her village—a live chicken, duck or a chunk of homemade ham—and Ada always would make sure that a gift of cash was ready for her when she departed after a few days' stay.

A month before my wet nurse terminated her employment, Ada hired a nanny from a nearby village to take care of me. She was in her early forties, and I called her "Mamma Chang." Her marriage had turned into a loveless relationship many years before when she discovered that her husband had taken up with a much younger woman. In addition to his affair, he had a bad drinking problem. When their daughter turned seventeen and married, Mamma Chang decided it was time to leave her unhappy home and, to support herself, she took the job as my nanny. Ada immediately liked Mamma Chang's "no nonsense" appearance. With her hair pulled back from her angular face into a tight little bun, she looked clean and crisp, exuding an air of certainty and precision. By the time my wet nurse left, I had already bonded with Mamma Chang. Life under her care had discipline and regularity. Each day she woke me up at eight in the morning, after she had been up for a couple of hours. I would get upset if I found out that she had been up first, so to appease me, she would return to her bed just prior to waking me up. As I got older, however, I also got smarter. When I saw her neatly combed bun, I knew that she had been up for a while. To make up for that betrayal, I would brattily demand that she let her hair down and recomb it all over again. After breakfast, I looked forward to visiting the family chicken and duck, which were kept in the bamboo garden in a little wooden house. I loved to collect the eggs they laid. Since they didn't lay eggs every day, I later learned that the breakfast cook would place two eggs in their nests each morning before I got there, so I was never disappointed. From an early age I adored animals, so the next stop was the horse stables. On our way there, we would pass the building where both the laundry was done and the chamber pots were cleaned. As we passed, the wash-women would drop their laundry and come over to greet me. Other than in our quarters, there were no modern flushing toilets on the compound, so chamber pots were in use everywhere else. The servants would clean them with detergent and handfuls of small clam shells, scrubbing them briskly with long bamboo whisks. Among the chamber pots there were dozens of special red lacquered pots which belonged to Mrs. Upstairs. She insisted that her pots be thoroughly cleaned and aired for a minimum of three days before being put back in service again, so there were always many extra red pots lined up outside the laundry building.

The breakfast cook supplied me with a basket of carrots and apples each day to take along to the stable as treats for the horses. By the time we arrived, the horses had usually returned from their workout with my father and uncle, and were being washed and groomed. I enjoyed feeding them the goodies and in a short time, as soon as they saw me in Mamma Chang's arms, they anticipated the treats. They were always very gentle with me. Once, my mother witnessed me sticking my tiny hand into a horse's mouth and she screamed with horror. I just pulled my hand back out and laughed at her.

After my visit to the stables, I would usually return to my room until my mother rose. Ada had an electric buzzer under her pillow, which she would ring when she awakened. I was trained not to make too much noise until the buzzer rang. Ada would wait in bed for a maid to bring her a glass of warm salt water for her to gargle, followed by a cup of tea and a very light breakfast. After we heard the buzzer, Mamma Chang would bring me into Ada's room to greet her. At eighteen months, I could talk, but was very wobbly on my feet. Apparently, my large head made my center of gravity very high. If anyone breathed too hard next to me, I would practically tip over—so Mamma Chang carried me around most of the time. I sat in my mother's bedroom on a small stool on the side of her bed and watched her taking her morning tea. A friend of Ada's had given me a box of cards, each of which had a word on one side and a corresponding picture on the other. One day, to pass the time, my mother showed me three cards and repeated each word three times. To her amazement, I remembered the three words the next morning. She taught me three more words and, soon, it became a routine. My education had begun.

One day, a relative who lived on the compound came to visit and Ada decided to show me off. She randomly pulled the cards out of the box, giving me a little pop-quiz. I answered rapidly, without any mistakes. Ada's visitor was duly impressed. She had a daughter only three months older than I, and she asked Ada if she could send her little girl over to be taught at the same time. Ada agreed, thinking that it would be good for me to have a classmate. The next morning, the little girl and her nanny arrived. She played with me in my room until the buzzer rang and we both were ushered into my mother's room. We sat quietly on stools while she finished her tea. Then, my mother started to teach us the three words for the day. Maybe the little girl was shy, or perhaps scared, but she had a very hard time with the first word. Ada tried and tried, repeating the word ten or fifteen times. Still, the little girl could not get it. Finally, Ada said to the child's nanny, I just don't have the patience for this. Please don't bring her back again." That was the end of my classmate, but I continued my daily lesson of three new words. Eventually, I finished three boxes of cards, with one hundred cards in each box.

Ever since my near-starvation under the care of the first wet nurse, Mother stayed around the house more often, fearing some other life threatening incident. The afternoon Mahjong game was regularly set up in our quarters. With me in her arms, Mamma Chang would stand behind Mother and watch the game. Sometimes, Ada would take advantage of the opportunity to show off her smart baby. She would show me a Mahjong tile and tell me what it was before she discarded it. The next time the same tile came up she would stop and ask me to identify it. I always gave her the correct answer, to the amazement of all the ladies at the table. It was not long before I could recognize every Mahjong tile in the set.

At twenty months, I came down with the measles. The episode caused much drama and anxiety, even though I recovered fairly quickly under the doctor's care. During my recuperation, relatives in the compound all gave Ada different advice about how she should take care of me. Many of the older ladies did not trust western medicine, but relied on their own home remedies, passed down from generations. Being inexperienced in raising children, Ada took bits of suggestions from here and there. One rule common to all the advice was not to let the child eat too much, in order to avoid digestive problems. Ada overdid it. She kept me on such a strict diet that I began to experience starvation for the second time in my short life. The weight loss once again exaggerated my oversized head and long skinny neck, giving me the appearance of a famine survivor.

Around that time, Ada's older sister, Shan-dah, and her husband, Dr. Chou, came to visit Changchow. Uncle Chou, an orthopedic surgeon, was starting a medical practice in Shanghai after returning from the U.S. where he had completed advanced studies at Johns Hopkins University. Because they had been abroad for almost three years, this was the first time that Shan-dah and Chou had met me. Ada admired Uncle Chou's medical skills and asked him to give me a complete physical check up. Though he gave me a clean bill of health, he recommended that I be fed extra nutritious food and plenty of it. He also strongly suggested that I be circumcised, for future hygienic purposes. Immediately, I was taken to the facility next door, the hospital my grandfather built, and Uncle Chou performed the operation.

While living on the compound, Ada always made monthly shopping trips to Shanghai. She bought presents for her mother, Ivy, Mrs. Upstairs, my father, my uncle, my nanny and some of her favorite servants. The majority of the presents, however, were for me. Once she purchased so many toys—including a life-sized rocking horse—that a luggage car had to be chartered to carry all the goodies to Changchow.

Aunt Jill visited so often that it seemed like she was almost a regular family member. Though she never acquired the habit of playing Mahjong, she did enjoy watching the game and participating in the chitchat going on around the table. While the other women played, Aunt Jill would knit, her busy needles producing sweaters, hats, pants, socks and blankets for me. My extensive wardrobe of hand-knitted goods was the envy of everyone. Being slightly plump, she also took pleasure in the constant snacking that went on during the game. Jill had the habit of eating a lot and then running to the bathroom to purge, but no one then had heard of bulimia.

Another frequent visitor was Aunt Hwa, who had been a classmate of Ada's and Jill's in the midwife school at the China Convalescent Hospital. She was a most unusual sight for the 1930s, and particularly unusual for Changchow—she always wore men's clothing and sported a man's haircut. Though Ada and other friends tried to fix her up, Auntie Hwa never got married. From a poor family, she had taken a job as a midwife in Shanghai to support herself, but spent much of her time at our compound, a three-hour train trip from the city.

Miss No. 1 and Miss No. 2 were also regular visitors to the compound, arriving with their sons in tow and a staff of four servants each. Our household had plenty of guests, and the compound was always filled with excitement and social activities. The summer villa my father was building on beautiful Horseshoe Island was nearing completion. Ada's love for her husband was also growing as the days went by—the marriage had turned out to be ideal after all. Ada felt that her life was now perfect, and was confident it would be always. The good life, it seemed, was here to stay.

Chapter Thirteen ─────────

Japan invaded and occupied Manchuria, the three provinces in the northeast corner of China, adjacent to Siberia, in 1931. The area was rich with gold, iron and many other ores, and was an important stepping stone for Japan in its imperialist goals throughout Asia. The Japanese renamed this territory Manchuquo and established it as an independent country, separate from China. To appease the Chinese people and other world powers, Japan brought the Last Emperor of China to Manchuria to function as a puppet ruler under the close scrutiny of the Japanese military. The Japanese then began to expand their territory southward, slowly at first. Finally, they openly declared war against the Chinese Republic.

By 1937, Japanese troops had invaded and occupied Peking, the former capital of the Ching Dynasty, and every day we heard the news that the invading troops were moving southward. Ada began to fear that the Japanese would soon reach Changchow. As the battle zone drew nearer, she told Zee that she thought the family should move to Shanghai—at least temporarily. Ada felt that Shanghai, an international city, would be safe from military attack unless the Japanese were prepared for a war with England or France. Zee, on the other hand, was extremely optimistic. He didn't believe that Japanese troops would ever venture south of the Yangtse River, where Changchow lay. If she was truly nervous about the political situation, however, Ada and the baby should visit Shanghai. Since she had not been feeling up to par, Ada reasoned that a few weeks of pampering at the China Convalescent Hospital would be good for her. I was barely two years old when mother packed up me and Mamma Chang for a trip to Shanghai. As we prepared our bags, father saw Mamma Chang trying to stuff a silk quilted jacket she had just had made into her suitcase. He told her she was crazy to take a winter jacket on a midsummer trip and asked her whether she planned to stay through the New Year season. Mamma Chang took his advice and left her new winter jacket behind. We ended up taking one suitcase full of summer clothes for each of the three of us. Father was certain that in a few months "this war thing" would blow over. He saw us off at the train station and made sure the most important item—a watermelon, my favorite fruit—was put in our compartment should I want it on the trip. When the train started to move, Ada's parting words to Zee were, "Take good care of my mother!"

As we waved good-bye to Zee, little did we know that we would never again see many of those we left behind. Nor did we imagine that we were leaving a way of life which had prevailed in our family for twenty generations, but which would soon become but a memory.

Part Two: Shanghai

Chapter Fourteen ────────────

S hanghai, originally a sleepy fishing village, was one of five cities along the coast of China, portions of which were turned over to European powers after China lost the Opium Wars. The English and French "Concessions," zones of Shanghai which were exempt from Chinese authority, had dominated the city since the 1830s. The United States, which was not getting an equivalent share of Shanghai trade, eventually called for an "Open Door Policy." The U.S. prevailed and, soon, Shanghai opened up for international trade and settlement, without many restrictions or regulations. By the 1920s, Shanghai had emerged as a glamorous international city, the fourth largest in the word, rivaling Paris, London, and New York. Chinese from all provinces mingled with foreigners from all parts of the world. European planners and architects designed most of the buildings in the International Settlement, rendering Chinese-style architecture only in the Chinese territory. Restaurants served every type of international cuisine, and western entertainment and night clubs were everywhere, earning Shanghai a reputation as "The City that did not sleep" or just plain, "The Sin City."

When we arrived, Ada took me and Mamma Chang directly to

the home of her friends, Mr. and Mrs. Nu. Mr. Nu was the prosperous owner of a construction company and had purchased a large plot of land at the outer edge of the International Zone, adjacent to a vast expanse of farm land. He designed and built for himself a large mansion with beautiful gardens in the front and back. The house itself was a two-story red brick building with eight bedrooms, not including the servants' quarters. Mrs. Nu was a very fashionable lady who wore high heels everywhere—her bedroom slippers even had high heels. The Nus had five children, ranging from twelve to a six-month-old infant. The first and last were boys, with three girls in between. My mother arranged for Mamma Chang and me to be house guests of the Nus while she checked into the China Convalescent Hospital to enjoy some pampering. The first evening there I fussed all night because of the strange surroundings. I kept asking to go to the stables to see the horses, and wouldn't stop crying. By the next day, however, after playing with the other children and enjoying it immensely, I felt totally at home.

On the third night, Mamma Chang and I were in the large double bed in our bedroom, which was directly across the hall from the nursery where the baby boy slept with his wet nurse. Since the house was right on the border of the city, we could hear the Japanese aircraft bombing nearby Chinese territories. We had grown accustomed to both the engine noises of the Japanese planes and the antiaircraft guns which the Chinese troops, stationed just outside the city limits, fired throughout the night. Sometimes the male servants climbed onto the roof to watch the air combat in the distance. Even though there seemed to be more planes in the sky than usual and the antiaircraft guns were sending out a continuous barrage of ammunition that night, I still fell sound asleep when my head hit the pillow, like any two-year old. Later that night, Mamma Chang suddenly heard a chilling scream, followed by a continuous loud moan. She rushed out of the room. The hallway was full of people who were also trying to locate this ungodly moan. Soon they realized that the sound was coming from the nursery across the hall. Mr. Nu and the servants charged into the room. The sight they came upon was unreal.

The entire room was covered with broken plaster and there

was a large hole in the ceiling. In bed, the wet nurse, with her eyes closed, was moaning loudly. Next to her, the infant boy, covered with pieces of plaster, was miraculously still asleep. Mr. Nu immediately grabbed the baby and ran to a phone to call an ambulance. No one could figure out what happened, since there was not an open wound or blood on the wet nurse. When the ambulance arrived and the paramedics took the wet nurse out on a stretcher, a fourteen-inch-long antiaircraft shell was discovered under her body. The shell was a dud which hadn't exploded in the sky as usual, but had come down through the roof. It hit the wet nurse in the chest and the impact was fatal. She died on her way to the hospital. A bomb squad arrived soon after to remove the shell.

Ada went into a state of panic when she heard the news. She immediately contacted Miss No. 2, my father's sister, and asked if we could stay with her. Miss No. 2 and her husband lived in a three-story town house on a double lot in the middle of the fashionable French Concession. Miss No. 2 agreed, so Ada checked out of the hospital and moved into the third floor of the townhouse with me and Mamma Chang. By our seventh day in Shanghai, the Japanese had bombed out the railroad into the city. The news of the war was erratic, and what we did hear was all bad. Japanese soldiers had crossed the Yangtse River and had taken Nanking, the capital city of Chiang Kai-Shek's government. The infamous "Rape of Nanking," as the attack was called, was a bloody slaughter that shocked China and the world. We knew that Changchow would be the next city after Nanking, and feared the worst. Soon we received word that our family compound had been bombed. Ada was devastated. Even worse than the news we did hear was our inability to contact the family. All communication lines were down. Ada's worry about family members, especially about Zee and her mother, caused such anxiety that her hair turned gray. She was only twenty-eight years old when she started tinting her hair. We waited for four more months, without any news.

Chapter Fifteen ───────────────

When Zee heard about the fall of Nanking, he finally accepted that Changchow would be the next Japanese target. Young and patriotic, both Zee and his brother, Chi, threw themselves completely into the war effort. Working without sleep for days on end, they opened the family warehouses of rice and dried goods for the many thousands of refugees, needing food and clothing, who had escaped from the Nanking area, and turned the family hospital over to the wounded Chinese soldiers coming from the front lines. Mrs. Upstairs, Mrs. Lee, Ivy and all the women and children of the other families were sent to the nearly completed summer villa on Horseshoe Island. Most of the servants, preferring to move with their masters rather than returning to the war-torn countryside, also went to the island. Over one hundred people soon settled on the island, each person carrying with them their most valuable possessions, and Zee and Chi shipping several months of food supplies.

Father and Uncle Chi stayed in Changchow, working feverishly in the hospital and refugee center. The city, filled with desperate people, was in complete chaos. Japanese planes flew overhead, dropping bombs day and night. The hospital was the tallest building in town and the compound was the largest building complex, which made them obvious targets for the bombers. Soon, the entire compound was bombed, with fires lasting several days. Priceless antiques, art work, gold, silver, clothing and precious jewels, collected over many generations, including personal gifts from the Chinese emperors, were now just ashes.

Zee and Chi stayed on in Changchow even after the bombing. They were working in the open field helping the wounded when word came that Japanese soldiers were only an hour away from Changchow. Everyone feared that the horrific fate of Nanking would also befall Changchow so, as the soldiers approached, a massive tide of people rushed out of the city, hoping to escape to the southeast. At the last possible moment, Father and Uncle Chi hid cash in their pockets and changed into peasants' clothing. They merged into the huge flow of humanity escaping the city on foot. As they crossed the city limits, they heard loud Japanese gunfire coming from the other end of town. They walked for many days and finally reached Ningpo, where they secured boat passage south along the China coast to Hong Kong. It wasn't long before Japan drove the Chinese soldiers inland and occupied the entire eastern coast of China. When the battle zones moved inland, Father and Uncle Chi felt it was safe for them to return to Shanghai by boat since the coastal areas, although governed by the Japanese, were no longer threatened by military attack.

During and after the Japanese attacks on Changchow, the group of people who had settled on Horseshoe Island were the subject of widespread rumors. People speculated that the women and children had taken an immense fortune to the island. Since all law and order had broken down during the war, groups of bandits began to raid the island. With guns and knives, and sometimes even sickles and hoes, they charged into the villa, robbing family members of money, gold, and other valuables. These attacks happened over and over until there was little left to appease the bandits. Grandmother Lee had only one simple gold band left on her hand and begged the bandits not to take it. Nevertheless, they roughly pulled it off her finger. Soon after, she fell ill. The constant fear, frustration, hopelessness, and desperation, combined with her old age, made her lose her will to live. A boil formed behind her shoulder and an infection set in. There were no doctors or medication on the island

and she soon fell into a coma. She died a few days later, and was given a primitive burial in a hidden grave on the island. When the war zone finally moved further inland, the survivors managed to send a message to Shanghai. My father and uncle had recently arrived in the city and they immediately went back to the island to move our family to Shanghai. The other families, which had lived on the compound and then on the island disbanded, most of them going their own separate way. Mrs. Upstairs, her personal maid, and of course Ivy and her nanny moved in with us. Ada and Zee were happy at being reunited, but it was a sad and trying time. Ada was devastated over the loss of her mother and blamed herself for not bringing Grandma Lee with her when she came to Shanghai. No amount of tears or self-blame, however, could turn back the clock. We had been luckier than many—entire families had perished during the war. Human life seemed worth very little in such desperate times.

Chapter Sixteen

Though our family was together again, for the first time in generations we had no money and few valuables to convert to cash. The five members of our family and three servants all moved into Miss No. 2's fifteen-room townhouse in Shanghai. The quarters were crowded, given Miss No. 2's own large household. To add to the discomfort, Miss No. 2's husband happened to be a fanatic about cleanliness. He didn't work, so was home all day and would follow everyone around, dusting and wiping up after them. The first moment he could, my father went to the President of "Success Textiles" in Shanghai, the company in which my grandfather had invested many years ago. He asked him to reissue the family's stock certificates since the original ones were burned when the compound was bombed. As soon as he received the certificates, Father sold enough shares for us to lease a townhouse in a development called "Bubbling Well Villa," located on Bubbling Well Road (changed to Nanking Road West later) in the busy central region of the English Concession. After the frightening incident at the Nu residence near the border, Ada wanted to live close to the center of the city.

With its British and French Concessions, Shanghai was a unique Chinese city. You could easily tell which area you were in by looking at the policemen. The English sector had all Indian policemen, whose uniforms were topped with red turbans. In the French sector, the policemen were Vietnamese, wearing navy blue berets. Despite the Japanese occupation of the Chinese area of Shanghai, there was virtually no military presence in the International Zone. When the Chinese troops which had ringed the International Settlement were defeated, they withdrew, so there was nothing to stop the Japanese from entering and ransacking, burning, raping and killing as they had done elsewhere. Perhaps fearing foreign intervention, however, the Japanese government ordered that no destruction was to take place in the foreign section of Shanghai. A small contingent of Japanese soldiers peacefully entered the area, with a larger number of soldiers stationed outside the border. Unlike so much of the rest of the country, Shanghai was mercifully spared from being turned into a charred ruin. Within weeks of the Japanese occupation, business, entertainment, and life in general in Shanghai returned to normal.

In early 1938, we settled into Bubbling Well Villa, a development of row upon row of identical three-story red brick attached European styled townhouses. The entry to our house was a pair of wrought iron gates which opened into a small courtyard, leading to the front door. The first floor consisted of a living room, dining room, very small kitchen, powder room and an attached one-car garage. The second and third floors each had two large bedrooms, a smaller bedroom and a bath. There were also servants' bedrooms on the two landings between floors, and a sizable roof deck. My parents occupied a large bedroom on the second floor, which had a small balcony off of it, large enough for two small chairs. Mamma Chang and I had the other large bedroom on the second floor, and Ivy slept in the smaller bedroom on the same floor. Ivy's nanny had returned to her village because Ivy insisted that, at eight, she was old enough not to have a nanny following her around. My Uncle Chi and Mrs. Upstairs each took a large bedroom on the third floor. Mrs. Upstairs' personal maid slept in the same room in order to help Mrs. Upstairs' with her midnight trip to the bathroom. My father signed a long term lease on the house and hired a live-in cook and maid. He also purchased a new winter wardrobe for everyone. We began to feel as though we were living a normal life again, but one which was drastically different than before.

My father had hoped to attain a managerial position at "Success Textiles," but the managing principals fought to keep him out, afraid to lose their control of the company. Father decided to ignore these power-hungry men and compete with them by starting his own business. With the proceeds of the sale of five percent of "Success Textiles" stock, plus a bank loan, he bought a small textile factory which was on the verge of bankruptcy. He totally focused on making the new venture profitable, working long hours six days a week.

Chi, however, still had no interest in working for a living. He stayed in bed until noon every day and, in the evenings, made the rounds of the many ballrooms and nightclubs which thrived in Shanghai. The first-rate nightclubs had elegant Art Deco settings and served gourmet European cuisine. Influenced by the latest Hollywood films, some of these night spots looked like the kind of place where Fred Astaire and Ginger Rogers might step onto the dance floor at any moment. The less exclusive ballrooms featured giant dance floors, where hundreds of couples took to the parquet floors nightly. These establishments also supplied hostesses to dance with gentlemen without partners. They were "taxi dancers," or, as the Chinese called them, simply "dance-girls." A man usually gave a dance girl a ticket for each dance, or gave her a string of tickets as a tip if he particularly liked her. Or, he could pay enough to cover an entire evening and take a girl on a date to a first class nightclub. My Uncle Chi was a regular customer of these places. He received an allowance from my father but often ran short of cash, and arguments between them would erupt over Chi's spending habits.

Ada had very few social engagements due to our tight financial status. She focused on her motherly responsibilities, enrolling Ivy in a nearby private school and starting regular daily lessons for me in reading and Arabic numerals. At two, I became a whiz at flipping picture blocks quickly and precisely. Ada also took time to sit down and have long talks with Ivy, providing quality time for the two of them. She wanted an amiable sibling relationship between Ivy and me, and instilled in Ivy the idea that, as an older sister, she should always love and protect her baby brother. It was as though she was a second mother to me. Ada successfully brought out the mother instinct in eight-year-old Ivy, who had no real mother of her own. For me, Ada used a different tactic. Telling me that I was fortunate to have a mother who loved me more than her own life, she convinced me to share whatever goodies I received with Ivy. So instead of fighting over everything like other siblings, Ivy and I always tried to give whatever we received to the other. Due in very large part to the efforts of our mother, Ivy and I developed a good relationship early in our lives.

Father's new textile venture, the "New China Spinning Mills" was remarkably successful within the first couple years. To ward off inflation, Father put most of the profits from the business into real estate. In addition to our own home in Bubbling Well Villa, he bought four medium-size houses in a fashionable part of the French sector and two large houses in the English sector. For the time being, he leased out all six houses to produce income. Ada liked the four French Concession houses very much. They were built with high quality construction and their clustered layout created a large common garden in the middle. She hoped one day to combine the four, making two very large houses with a large garden in between. She dreamed that one of the combined houses would become her home with her husband, and the other would house her son and his family. She even envisioned a glassed-in walkway linking the two houses, so she wouldn't have to brave the weather if she wanted to visit her grandchildren. First, however, the war would have to end. Until then, all hopes and dreams for the future were on hold.

Chapter Seventeen ────────────

In the summer of 1939, I turned four years old, and my mother decided to enroll me that fall in the school Ivy attended. Even in Shanghai, there was no public educational system and the private schools cost more than an average family could afford. Ada enrolled me in kindergarten at Ivy's school, and returned home with a bag of school supplies—picture books, crayons and a bib. My Father and Uncle Chi showed me the books and, proudly, I read all the words and pictures from the first page to the last, with no mistakes. They were outraged that the level was so far below my capability. Zee sent Ada back to the school to change my enrollment, insisting that I should be put into the second grade. She followed his instructions and changed the enrollment, but after she returned, a few visiting friends told her they were astonished that she would put a four-year old child into the second grade. They felt that it could be damaging to push me too hard. So Ada raced back to the school and changed me back to kindergarten. Once again Father was upset. Finally, they compromised and she enrolled me in the first grade—refusing to change her mind again, no matter what anyone said.

The first day of school, Ada and Mamma Chang walked with me and Ivy the few blocks to school. Soon after we arrived, Ada said good-bye and left. Mamma Chang put me in my seat and I started to cry, holding on to her sleeve and refusing to let go. The teacher assured me that Mamma Chang could stay in the classroom with me, but she had to sit at the back of the room. When I finally let go and Mamma Chang moved to the back, I turned around every few minutes to make sure she was still there. She was not alone. There were half a dozen nannies sitting in the classroom, most of them passing the time by sewing or knitting. Finally, I settled down, knowing Mamma Chang was there to stay. Mamma Chang remained at school with me until I reached third grade and nannies were no longer allowed in a classroom. After walking both Ivy and me to school, she would sit in my classroom and make quilted winter shoes for us. At recess, I would spend the entire time with her, too shy to make friends with the other students, who all looked so much bigger than I. At noon, we would fetch Ivy and all walk home for lunch together. School days were long—from eight in the morning until four in the afternoon with a half day on Saturday.

I knew how to read all the first grade books before I started school, so my grades that year were the best in the class. In the second grade, however, I had to learn new words and to take math. School was no longer "a piece of cake." Until that time, I had thought that I would always know every word and every answer during an examination. One day, during a test, I forgot how to write a word and panic set in. I started to cry. Mamma Chang came to my seat and asked what was wrong. I told her that I had forgotten how to write a particular word. Since she was totally illiterate she couldn't help, so she grabbed the test paper of the little girl across the aisle from me and showed it to me. The stunned teacher just glared at us, not sure what to do. A little while later, I had trouble with another word. Again, I cried. This time, however, the teacher was prepared. She motioned for Mamma Chang to stay put, and then asked me which word I was having trouble with. I told her and she wrote the word on the blackboard, figuring, I suppose, that it was better this way than having my nanny grab another student's test paper. Mamma Chang, of course, reported the incident to my mother. By now, Ada had once again developed a very busy social schedule and didn't have much time to help me with my homework. Since none of the servants knew how to read or write, Ada decided to hire my teacher, Miss Ling, as a tutor for both Ivy and me. Every evening, Monday through Friday, Miss Ling would arrive promptly at six. She would sit at the table between Ivy and me while we did homework until eight. Then we all had dinner together. After dinner, Miss Ling departed and we got ready for bed. With her help, I soon regained my place at the top of the class. Ivy, however, disliked being tied down every evening. She passively resisted, giving Miss Ling the silent treatment. No matter what she said, Ivy wouldn't respond. Miss Ling was very frustrated and spoke to Ada about it. Ada always felt awkward disciplining Ivy, so she discussed the problem with Zee. Holding the traditional belief that education was not important for a girl, Zee convinced Ada that if Ivy didn't want a tutor, she didn't have to have one. From then on, Ivy's evening hours were free, though I was still at the dining room table with my tutor every night. The result was that I was always among the top three in my class while Ivy dropped to the bottom third of hers,

Ada usually arranged to spend time with Ivy and me on Sundays, planning her Sunday social events after six p.m. On Sunday mornings, she would often take us to the large department stores on Nanking Road. Elegant and impressive, these stores had carpeted floors, played soft music, and scents from the cosmetic department wafted throughout the store. The elevator operators were pretty girls, wearing uniforms. One store had installed the first and only escalator in China, and I loved riding up and down on it. The biggest attraction for us, however, was the children's department. Almost every time we went shopping, my mother would buy us each a few things. Ivy usually wanted clothing. I preferred books rather than toys. Ada was happy that I was interested in books, and bought me volumes of Chinese ghost stories, as well as Chinese translations of classics like Aesop's Fables.

Our daily meals were always pure Chinese dishes prepared by our cook. It was a particular treat on Sundays, therefore, when Ada would take us to a western restaurant for lunch. Learning to eat with forks and knives was great fun for Ivy and me. We would sample the food at Russian, German, English and French restaurants. I particularly loved the hot borscht at the Russian restaurant, which was served with a big glob of sour cream. After lunch, we usually took in a movie. I was easily frightened by the movies and had nightmares for weeks after seeing films like *The Wizard of Oz* and *Snow White and the Seven Dwarfs*. The gunfire and fist fights of the Westerns also scared me, and I was bored with dramas. Ada soon discovered that the only movies I could sit through without boredom or subsequent nightmares were musicals. That was the beginning of my lifelong fondness for Hollywood musicals, especially the ones in Technicolor.

After the movie, Ivy and I usually complained about being hungry. To us, western lunches just didn't stay with you like Chinese food did. Perhaps that was because we never ate the potatoes or vegetables served with the meal, thinking it was just decoration. The only Western restaurant we found completely satisfying was one which was owned by a Chinese family. At the end of each meal, they always brought out a large plate of fried rice. To appease our afternoon hunger, Ada would take us to tea at a fancy European coffee shop. One Belgian coffee shop, Bianchi's, featured fabulous pastries, and three others nearby, D.D.'s, Sullivan's, and Keisling's, were all excellent. Ivy and I were not allowed to have coffee or tea so we always ordered our favorite ice cream sodas, strawberry for Ivy and vanilla for me. Neither of us particularly liked sweet cakes or pastries, so instead we usually had little two-inch square double decker club sandwiches. They were made with thinly sliced and trimmed square bread, cut into four pieces. Ivy and I together could easily polish off half a dozen of these petite sandwiches.

Since Ivy was six years older than I, she soon wanted to walk to and from school with her friends, rather than with her baby brother and his nanny. So, Mamma Chang and I walked the few blocks alone together every day. At the beginning of December, 1941, I was finishing the fall semester of the third grade, and the weather had turned very cold. One morning, as Mamma Chang walked me to school as usual, she held my hand as she always did with her right hand and carried my books in her left hand. When we were within a half block of the school, someone came up behind her and tapped her on the shoulder. She turned around. A man handed her an envelope and said, "Here is a very important letter.

Please take it to your Master."

Mamma Chang said yes, and let go of my hand to accept the envelope. In that split second, I disappeared. All Mamma Chang saw was a car speeding away from the curb and me sitting in the lap of a man in the front passenger seat. The man who had handed her the envelope quickly turned and ran alongside the car. He leaped onto the running board and hooked his arm through the open window, as the car sped around the corner. Mamma Chang screamed and collapsed onto the sidewalk. Illiterate, she couldn't even read the numbers on the license plate. It had happened so fast, and her wailing was so incomprehensible that no one on the street realized what had just taken place. Mamma Chang's legs went weak from shock and she couldn't rise from the sidewalk. She cried and screamed, crawling toward our home. Passersby stepped around her without offering any help—thinking that Mamma Chang was a crazy woman. When she arrived home, she was still crying and screaming at the top of her lungs. My parents, awakened by the commotion, ran down the stairs to see what had happened. Mamma Chang still could not speak. Totally incomprehensible wails and cries were all that she uttered. Ada tried to calm her down. Finally, Father saw the envelope she was tightly clutching in her hand. He opened it and read the short note-"We've got your boy! Don't worry, we'll take good care of him. You'll be contacted by someone soon." It was just a few days before Japan attacked Pearl Harbor, and I was kidnapped.

Chapter Eighteen ─────────

Shanghai had been occupied by the Japanese since 1937 but the wartime economy in the city was amazingly robust. Success Textiles, the company in which my Grandfather had invested, was booming. It had expanded to nine factories, and our stock provided dividends for my family of many times more than we could ever spend. My Uncle Chi was perfectly happy not working and living a playboy's life on his share of the income. My Father's business, the New China Spinning Mills, also began turning a good profit by 1939. Within two years of the immense loss in Changchow, Father had swiftly recovered and once again reached the ranks of the very rich. He tried to live an unassuming lifestyle during the war, however, not wanting to attract attention to his wealth. We continued to live in the small, crowded townhouse, but he hoped that one day the Japanese would be defeated and we could again return to the kind of life we had enjoyed before the war.

Meanwhile, Ada's stepmother, A-do, in Wusi, had fallen on hard times financially. Because of her expensive opium habit, she had been forced to sell the big house with the impressive spiral staircase and move to a meager rooming house. With three sons to raise, the money she received from the sale of the house did not last very long. Opium had been legalized during the Japanese occupation and was even more available than it was before the war. A-do continued to sell everything she had to support her drug habit.

One day, her eldest son, a tall and handsome twenty year old, appeared at our front door. He asked for assistance, and Zee gave him a managerial position at the New China Spinning Mills. Father also rented a room for him near the factory and bought him a new wardrobe. Ada's young, patriotic half-brother would usually spend every weekend at our home and would talk constantly about how much he hated living under Japanese control. Finally, he decided to join Chiang Kai-shek's Chinese Republican army. To reach their headquarters in Chungking, he had to first make it across the battle lines. My parents tried to warn him of the danger he would face, but failed to talk him out of his plan, He was soon off to fight for his country, outfitted with clothing and cash supplied by my father. Unfortunately, he never made it to the Chinese side. We later learned that he was brutally killed by the Japanese near the front lines.

Early in 1941, A-do's second son showed up at our doorstep. Like his elder brother, he too was tall and handsome. My father offered him the same arrangement as his brother before him. One Sunday, when he was at our house for dinner, Ada noticed that he had on a pair of new leather-soled shoes, instead of the rubber soled ones she had just purchased for him. He confessed that he had exchanged the shoes because the rubber soles were not good for dancing. Ada realized then that he was frequenting the Shanghai dance halls and partaking of their assorted pleasures. She had a long talk with him, urging him not to throw away the opportunity my father had given him.

A few Sundays later, after he had once again been a dinner guest at our house, my father's gold wrist watch was missing from the top of his dresser. Since my mother completely trusted the household servants, she immediately suspected her half-brother. The next day he didn't show up for work at the factory. Ada went to his rooming house and discovered that he had moved out three days earlier. A week later, she received a phone call from him. He confessed that he had taken the gold watch and promised he would give her the pawn ticket if she would come and get it. Ada went to the lice-ridden flop house where he said he was staying. After stepping over many bodies passed out on the floor, she found him. He was high on drugs, but lucid enough to hand over the pawn ticket. Wanting to help him, she called Father and together they moved him to a hospital which had a drug rehabilitation treatment, checking him in for the duration of the cure. After several months, he was supposedly clean. My parents supplied him with funds, clothing and a one-way train ticket back to Wusi. Within days, however, he was back in Shanghai, though Zee and Ada didn't know it. Many of the Shanghai underworld figures at that time were natives of Wusi, and he soon became involved with the mob organization in the city. Eager to please his new bosses, he told them all about his half-sister and her wealthy husband, suggesting the perfect candidate for a kidnapping—me. Zee and Ada, he promised, would surely pay a large ransom for the return of their only son.

Chapter Nineteen

After Pearl Harbor Day, December 7, 1941, Japan was officially at war with the West. All English, French and American residents living in Shanghai were packed off to concentration camps in various locations to the west and south of the city. American movies and newsreels were banned, and residents had to turn in their shortwave radios for alteration, or risk being arrested as spies. Gasoline was restricted for military use only, so taxis were converted to wood-burning vehicles and private automobiles were outlawed. Unfortunately, only a few days before private cars were banned, I was kidnapped.

I was completely stunned when I was lifted off the sidewalk that day and hustled into the car. It happened so fast. I realized that I was in a strange car, but was too frightened to utter a sound. My mouth simply hung open in fear as the man in the passenger seat held me tightly in his lap. After the car careened around the corner, it stopped briefly so the man who was hanging onto the running board could get into the back seat. Finally, my lungs filled with enough air to let out a large gasp from the bottom of my chest. The man holding me told me not to be afraid.

"We are your friends," he said urgently. "The Japanese are raiding your house right now and your parents are on the run. We are going to hide you from the Japanese."

I still could not utter a word. Before long we drove through a pair of wooden gates into a driveway. The man in the back seat jumped out and closed the gates behind the car. The man who was holding me carried me into and through a completely empty house—not a stick of furniture. We reached a back room which finally had a single wooden chair, and he put me down on it. As soon as he released his grip, I jumped away and started running for the door. He quickly grabbed me and pulled me back. I struggled to get away, biting his hand with all my six-year-old strength and even drawing blood. While I fought for my freedom, another man, who was older, more distinguished-looking and dressed in a fine Western business suit, came into the room. He seemed very different from the three in the car. In an authoritative tone, he asked what was going on. The other man, who was by now holding both of my arms behind me, responded that I was giving him a hard time. The elegantly dressed man commanded him, "Go! Leave us alone!"

The first man left, nursing his bloody hand. I had a better feeling about this distinguished-looking one and let him pick me up and put me on his knees as he sat in the lone wooden chair. He spoke to me in a deep, gentle voice,

"We are at war with Japan. Your father, as you know, is an important man in the business world, and the Japanese have suddenly decided to arrest him. They've made up some insignificant charge, but it is obviously only an excuse to confiscate his lucrative business. Both of your parents are on the run and the only way to keep you safe without the Japanese finding you was for us to get you."

"But, I want to go home!" I cried, teary-eyed.

"You will. As soon as this thing blows over, I'll personally deliver you back home. For now, however, I want you to be a good boy so your parents will be proud of you."

My father rarely spoke more than one or two sentences to me during a day. It was a totally new experience for me to converse with a grown man. His gentle smile and soft voice soon began to win my confidence, though it is not that difficult, of course, to make a six-year-old believe a story. I wasn't completely satisfied with everything he had said, however. I pointed out to him that my parents were still asleep in bed when I left the house.

Again, he explained patiently, "They got a warning right after you left and had no time to do anything but get away. At the last minute they called me, asking if I would intercept you before you got to school, where the Japanese certainly intended to pick you up. I'm risking my life to hide you for a while. As soon as your parents reach the Chinese side, or another safe place, I will send you to join them."

During those chaotic years there were numerous stories about people being arrested, imprisoned and even executed. For a child living in an occupied city in the midst of the Second World War, this story sounded completely plausible. Even more important than his words, however, was the kindness in his voice. His tone made me feel I could trust him. He told me that the Japanese were already searching for me, so later, when we were to go out, I would have to be careful not to attract anyone's attention on the street, including the police. Noticing that I was calming down, he started to make small talk with me. He seemed to know everything about my family. We talked about Ivy, Mrs. Upstairs and Mamma Chang. (I was whisked away so fast, of course, that I had not seen Mamma Chang crying and screaming on the street.) He asked me about my school work and my likes and dislikes. I told him that I would love to have a dog, and he promised that one day he would give me one. When I told him how much I loved to sing, he asked me to tell him which songs I knew. I'm sure he expected me to list the usual popular children's songs. To his surprise, however, I named a bunch of love songs. Ivy always sang the popular tunes played on the radio, and I would learn the songs with her. I was thrilled when he asked me to sing a song for him. I had never had so much attention from a grown man in my whole life, and I just lapped it up. With much corny emoting, I performed one song after another. My impromptu concert seemed to last hours, as I regaled my kidnapper with my rendition of the current Chinese hit parade.

After a while, he called in the other three men and told them how smart I was. At one point he said he would love to have a son like me. Then he turned to me and said, "How about if I make you my godson, and you can call me 'Godfather' from now on?" He seemed genuinely fond of me. I thought for a moment and finally said, "I guess it's all right." Everyone cheered and congratulated us.

At home, praise from my parents was scarce, and this was the first time I had ever been the focus of so much adult praise and attention. I reveled in the moment. I loved feeling like I was being treated as an equal, rather than as a child. Godfather introduced me to the other three men. One of them said his name was Liu, the same last name as mine. He said that perhaps we were related and suggested that I address him as, "Cousin." I said, "O.K. Cousin!" The other two men were introduced as Ah Fong and Ah Loo. Ah Loo had a severe case of stuttering and, when I first heard him talk, I laughed uncontrollably. Ah Fong, whom I had bitten, was tall and lanky and the nicest looking of the four. I soon felt totally at ease with these men. Unlike at home, I was able to talk and voice my opinion whenever I wanted—I didn't have to refrain from speaking until I was spoken to. I was in Heaven!

After a while, Godfather said that they had to get me out of Shanghai, or the Japanese would surely find me. He showed me a box of clothing for my train trip, including a long woolen overcoat and a Russian hat. The hat, a wool felt cap with a convertible brim, was very common and used a lot in Shanghai during the winter season. When the brim was rolled down, it covered my whole face except the eyes, like a ski mask.

Since it was now past the noon hour, Ah Loo brought in lunch from a nearby restaurant. After lunch, I put on my new coat and hat and got into the car with the four men. When we reached the train station, Godfather pulled down the brim of my hat, held my hand, and we strolled at a leisurely pace toward the platform. Remembering what Godfather had said earlier, I lowered my eyes or looked away when I saw a policeman. The other three men stayed quite a distance from us, and even rode in a separate compartment. Godfather had brought along several story books for the trip—and I read them and chatted happily all the way to Hangchow.

Hangchow, located on a lake shore about three hours south of Shanghai by train, is an extraordinarily beautiful resort area. Usually it is filled with tourists, but winter is the off season so the city was fairly empty when we arrived. We settled into a resort hotel just a few blocks from the shoreline of the spectacular West Lake. From our rooms on the second floor, the magnificent lake looked like an enormous mirror surrounded by mountains. Godfather had a room of his own, and Ah Fong, Ah Loo, Cousin and I shared another very large room. There were three Chinese style canopy beds along three long walls of our room. I was assigned to one, Ah Fong and Ah Loo each chose one, and a rollaway bed was moved into the room for Cousin. A five-foot square dining table was in the center of the room, with eight dining chairs, two to each side. By now, it was evening. We had a large dinner sent to the room and Godfather came in to join us.

It had been a long, hectic day for me and I felt very sleepy after dinner. As I got ready for bed, I discovered that other cities were not as developed as Shanghai. Even in this first-class resort hotel, there were no toilets. The chamber pot was in an alcove with a curtain covering it, and the washing facility, halfway down the hall, had a sink with only cold water. A dozen large thermoses with hot water were lined against the wall near the sink. Since I was too little to lift the large thermoses, Ah Fong came to the washroom with me to help me wash my face. I was also surprised that there wasn't a bath tub in the washroom. Ah Fong explained that when I needed a bath, an attendant would bring a wooden tub into the bedroom and fill it with hot water for bathing. Since it was winter, however, and the hotel had no heating system—as was the case in most of China—he thought it would be better for us to go to the well-heated nearby public bath. That sounded great to me. I returned to the bedroom where Godfather was supervising Ah Loo, who was unpacking a suitcase filled with things for me—sweaters, shirts, jackets, long underwear, hats, scarves, gloves, pajamas and a heavily-quilted robe. Although I wanted to look at the new things, I was so sleepy that all I could do was crawl into bed. As I slipped under the covers, I thought about my parents and wondered where they were hiding out. I also thought about Mamma Chang. This was the first night since she had become my nanny that I had gone to bed without her gently patting me on the back until I started to doze off. My eyelids were so heavy, though, that I couldn't think about them very much.

"Maybe I'll think about them tomorrow," I said to myself, as I drifted into the sweet blackness of sleep.

Chapter Twenty ⎯⎯⎯⎯⎯⎯⎯⎯

After breakfast the next morning, Godfather told me that he had to leave for a few days with "Cousin." But first he counseled me, "I want you to be a good boy. Promise me that you'll listen to Ah Fong and Ah Loo. They'll take good care of you. When I come back, I'll bring you a present."

Waving good-bye to him as he left, I gave him my promise that I would be a good boy. Soon after, Ah Fong asked me if I would like to go boating on the lake. I was thrilled—I had never even been on a boat before. The three of us walked the few blocks to the lake shore and found a dock with dozens of row boats for hire. The boats were all about twenty-five feet long and of the same design. In the middle, where it was widest, each boat had two upholstered love seats about five-feet wide, facing each other. In between the love seats was a table with a teapot and teacups on it. The boatman, seated at the rear of the boat, did the rowing and also served the tea. Ah Fong hired a boat and discussed the itinerary with the boatman. We settled down in our seats with our tea and began our journey on the calm and clear water, gazing at the magnificent lake, surrounded by mountains on three sides. Half hidden in the hills were several temples and, in the distance on a peak, a seven-story pagoda, reflected in the lake. There were a couple of very long tree-lined causeways running across parts of the lake. They arched upward to form a bridge under which boats could pass. The weather that day was remarkably mild. The sun was shining and it was actually warm as we glided slowly and silently across the surface of the lake. I was mesmerized by the endlessly beautiful scenery. Hangchow and this lake became at that moment forever etched in my memory as one of the most beautiful spots on earth.

After about an hour and a half, we docked at the foot of a mountain. We got out of the boat and began walking up hundreds of stone steps. At the end of a twenty-minute climb, we came upon a Buddhist temple, with ornate red and gold decor. I was fascinated, having never seen a Buddhist temple in Shanghai or anywhere else. A monk gave us a tour of the temple and then led us into a dining room where we were served a vegetarian lunch. Since winter was the off-season for tourists, we were the only visitors. After lunch, we bought some nuts and fruits to snack on and returned to the boat. At three o'clock we docked at a second temple, where we had a special treat—a sweet hot cereal made from lotus roots— which I loved and which was another new experience for me. Just before the sun began to set, we landed at the dock where we had started that morning and walked back to our room. For dinner, we again ordered room service and feasted around our big table. I was thrilled that I could eat anything I liked, quite different from the way it was at home.

The next morning Ah Fong took me to the public bath. The entire place was filled with hot steam and seemed very nice and warm. As I peered into a very large room, however, I saw many naked men in and around a large pool, washing themselves. I had not expected it to be a community bath and, feeling shy, refused to go in. Ah Fong didn't try to force me. He requested a private room with a private bath. The tub in the private room was much smaller than the pool in the community room, but it was ample for three of us.

I was beginning to really enjoy the camaraderie and male bonding I was experiencing with these men. Our daily routine, unless it was raining, was boating on the beautiful West Lake. Ah Fong, whose hand I had bitten on the first day, had now become my favorite companion. I loved romping and tumbling with him, a kind of play I had never been able to do at home. In fact, I was having a ball. My parents and Mamma Chang quickly faded from my thoughts.

After a few days, Godfather returned. He had brought not just one, but dozens of presents. There were many books, a phonograph and a collection of records, including both Chinese popular songs and Peking Opera. I had told him that my mother took singing lessons to learn the arias, and that I knew how to hum a few, too. With all of these new things, Godfather hoped that I wouldn't be bored in the hotel room on a bad weather day.

Godfather would come and go from time to time, usually only staying one or two nights on a visit and each time bringing lots of presents for me. On his second trip, he brought me a puppy. I had told him that no matter how many times I asked, my father wouldn't let me have a dog. Father thought I should concentrate on my school work rather than spend my time playing with a dog. He also said there was not enough space for a dog in our crowded living quarters.

I was thrilled with my new puppy—he was just a mutt, but to me he was the most beautiful dog in the world. Godfather told me to give him a name. In those days, all of the chic people in Shanghai gave their dogs English names, so naturally I wanted to give my puppy an English name. I didn't know any English names, however, except "Charlie," and it seemed like every dog I knew that was owned by a Chinese family was named "Charlie." I decided it was much too common a name for my dog, and asked Godfather to give him an unique name. He suggested "Borrow". I'm not quite sure why—in retrospect, I wondered if maybe it was because I was "borrowed" from my parents—but I happily christened the dog Borrow. After only one day, Borrow, who was extremely smart, was paper-trained. He slept in bed with me, under the covers. Since the bed was too high for him to reach, I arranged several chairs and stools of different heights as makeshift stairs so he could get up and down to the bed. Borrow was definitely the best of all the gifts I received from Godfather.

The next time Godfather came, he brought an elderly man and introduced him to me as my tutor. Instead of playing all the time, Godfather felt I needed to keep up with my school work. The tutor worked with me on Mondays, Wednesdays and Fridays from four to six p.m. That still gave me enough time for an outing each day with Ah Loo and Ah Fong. Since the winter days were short, we would always be back at the hotel by four, when dusk would set in.

I was having such a good time in this new life that I actually hoped I wouldn't have to return home too soon. I particularly liked Godfather, who, like Santa Claus, gave me everything I asked for. One day he looked at me intently, and asked, "Would you like to stay with me always and not return to your parents?"

I hesitated. In my heart I wanted to say "Yes", but I also felt it was wrong. Finally, I said, "My parents would be very sad because they love me so much, and Mamma Chang, too."

He patted me on my head and dropped the subject.

Chapter Twenty-one

As time went by, I began to change from the shy, introverted child I was before my kidnapping into an outgoing and sociable little boy. At home, I had been brought up very traditionally. I was not allowed to run or jump in front of adults. I was constantly reminded that I should sit, stand and walk properly. I could only speak when spoken to. In these new circumstances, however, I could join in a conversation whenever I wanted. I could make Ah Loo crawl on the floor so I could ride him like a horse. Ah Fong would toss me high into the air when we roughhoused, making me laugh loudly and uncontrollably. Yet, because of my upbringing at home, I never stepped beyond the bounds of being a well behaved child.

Godfather returned for another visit and this time brought his girlfriend with him, a pretty, fashionable woman in her 20s who wore rather heavy make-up. She told me that although she was not married to Godfather yet, I should still call her "Godmother" to get in practice. I happily agreed and asked when they were going to get married. When she told me that she hoped their wedding would be soon, I jumped up and down with excitement. My mother had taken me to several weddings before, and I always envied the little boys who were ring bearers or train bearers in the ceremonies.

In fact, shortly after we arrived at the hotel in Hangchow, there was a wedding taking place on the premises. I begged Ah Loo and Ah Fong to let me go downstairs to see the festivities. They gave in and took me to the wedding reception for a half-hour before bringing me back to the room to go to bed. Now, I thought, this impending wedding between Godfather and his girlfriend could make my wish to be part of a wedding come true. So, I boldly asked her to let me be her ring bearer.

"Of course you can," she said enthusiastically. "As a matter of fact, you are the only one I would have."

I was elated. After that conversation, every time I saw Godfather I urged him to get married soon.

By January, the weather was getting colder. It would drizzle continuously for days, and we couldn't go out on our daily excursions. Confined to the hotel room, I got bored—even with all my toys, books, records and Borrow. To keep me occupied, Godfather hired a man to teach me to sing Peking Opera, since he knew I had already acquired a taste for this traditional performing art from listening to my mother take her lessons. To accompany me, the opera teacher would play a bamboo stringed instrument, the Hwooching, which sounded like a harsh violin. Since I was so young and still had a high soprano voice, I had to learn the girls' parts. I insisted that Ah Fong learn the male parts, so we could sing duets together.

We were totally hotel-bound in February due to the heavy snowfall that year. From our hotel window I could look down at the garden and the spectacular white scenery. There were a couple of large Chinese plum trees in the garden and one day they burst forth with a cloud of pale pink blossoms. The blossoms looked magnificent against the snowy background.

Regardless of all my diversions, being stuck in the hotel room every day was tedious. To keep me happy, Ah Fong hired an eight-year-old girl from a nearby village for me to play with. Her father dropped her off at the hotel each morning and picked her up every evening. At first, I was quite happy to have a new playmate but, after a few weeks, I got tired of her. Because she was a girl, she didn't know boys' games like marbles, and I soon lost interest in playing the board games she did know. Ah Fong finally told her father not to bring her anymore.

By March, the weather improved and we resumed our daily boating and mountain-climbing activities. For variety, Ah Fong and Ah Loo would rent bicycles instead of a boat. I would ride in a seat behind one of them with Borrow in my arms. They told me that the bicycles were more economical than hiring a boat for a whole day, and it soon became obvious that they were on a frugal budget now. My opera teacher was terminated, and eventually my tutor also stopped coming. We would bring food with us for picnics rather than eating at restaurants and temples. None of this mattered to me. I was perfectly happy riding bicycles around the lake shore and the causeways. We would also fly kites and take long walks in the hills to hidden streams and waterfalls. With the spring sunlight, the flowering peach and weeping willow trees, which lined the causeway and shore for miles, began to bud. As the first warm days came, they finally displayed their new foliage and flowers in full glory. Along with the blossoms, tourists in great numbers also started to arrive at the resort hotels.

One day, Godfather returned, bringing a box of new clothes for the warmer weather. He took me to a photo studio and had several pictures taken of me in my new spring outfit. Godfather said that he might see my parents soon and he wanted to show them how good I looked. That evening, he asked me to write a letter to my parents. Since it was my first attempt at a real letter, I needed help. I worked hard, writing with extra care to show off my improved penmanship. The next day Godfather went boating with us for the first time. After we docked at a landing, we ascended a steep hill to a Buddhist temple. At this temple, for a fee, you could have your fortune told. You knelt in front of a statue of Buddha and held a large bamboo cup in your hand with a bundle of bamboo sticks in it. As you prayed, you shook the cup harder and harder until one of the sticks fell out of the cup. The stick was numbered. The monk in charge would then pull a sheet of paper with a corresponding number out of the file. The poem on that piece of paper was your fortune. Godfather, Ah Fong and Ah Loo all took their turns and seemed happy after reading their poems. Even though the meaning of the poems was beyond my comprehension, they told me to get my fortune as well. For some reason, I have remembered the poem I received that day throughout my life. It was written in the classical Chinese style with four sentences of seven words each. Essentially, it translated as:

The new moon reflects in the ocean like a silver hook.
It startles the fishes darting in the sea.
The moon sets, the hook disappears, the water becomes calm
The happy fishes are worry free.

I didn't know why then, but everyone thought that this was an especially good fortune for me.

The following day Godfather and Ah Fong departed, leaving Ah Loo as my lone keeper. Because it was the tourist season and the cost was so much higher, we didn't take any more boat rides. We did, however, take lots of long walks with Borrow, who had grown rapidly in size. He was now almost as big as a retriever.

One day, about a week after Ah Fong left, Ah Loo suggested a walk along the lake shore, but insisted on leaving Borrow in the hotel room. This seemed very unusual because Borrow always went everywhere with us. Ah Loo was adamant about not taking the dog, however, so I finally gave in. After we left the hotel, we headed in the opposite direction from the lake. I asked Ah Loo where we were going and he just shushed me. We turned a corner, where he hailed a rickshaw and told the puller to take us to the train station.

"The train station?" I yelled. "Why are we going to the station?"

"We are going to Shanghai," he said in a hushed tone. "I'll explain everything once we're on the train, but, for now, you must be quiet."

After we boarded the train, he told me that the hotel bill had not been paid for several weeks, so he had to go to Shanghai to get some money. All I could think of was my poor dog alone in the hotel room and I started to cry. He assured me that Borrow would be all right until tomorrow when we returned with the money. There was nothing I could do, and onward we went to Shanghai.

When we arrived, we took a rickshaw to a neighborhood which was completely unfamiliar to me, in a poor and rundown part of the city. We entered a house occupied by a woman and her three children, two boys and a girl. She fed us dinner that night and put us up in a tiny little bedroom. The next morning, Ah Loo left to take care of business while I played with the children. Even though they were slightly older than I, because they were poor, they didn't attend school. With my newly acquired social skills, I had a good time playing with them. In the afternoon, at one of the boys' suggestion, we played in the street. At the curb, several rickshaws were lined up, waiting for fares. For a split second, I thought I should hail a rickshaw to take me home. Then I realized, if my parents were really hiding, there might not be anyone at the house. So, I dropped the idea as fast as I picked it up and continued playing with my new friends.

When Ah Loo returned and saw me playing in the street, he turned pale. He started stuttering so badly that no words came out of his mouth. Grabbing my hand, he quickly took me into the house. We hastily said good-bye to the woman and headed for the train station. Once we were back in Hangchow, we checked into a small room in a different hotel, which had to be much cheaper than the other hotel. After dinner, Ah Loo put me to bed and left to pay the bill and fetch our belongings from the first hotel. In response to my urgent pleading, he promised to bring back Borrow. I was so tired, however, that I couldn't stay awake for his return.

When I woke up the next morning, all my toys, books, phonograph records and clothes were piled up in one corner—but there was no dog. Ah Loo told me that the hotel staff claimed the dog had run away. Very upset, I cried for a long time. Finally, I had to accept the fact that Borrow was gone.

A few days later, we were walking through Hangchow and passed by a little shop. The storekeeper was sitting outside the front door eating a bowl of rice. A stray dog sat in front of him, waiting for a handout. It was him! I immediately cried out, "Borrow!" He turned around and ran up to me, jumping all over me and almost knocking me down. He was dirty, hungry and limping from an injury to one of his front paws, but I couldn't stop hugging him. Finally we took him back to the hotel and fed him. Since there was no facility there for me to bathe him, I brushed him thoroughly with a stiff-bristled brush. He soon looked much better. After a few days of daily brushings, he was almost presentable. His injury quickly healed and he once again accompanied us on our long walks in the countryside, visiting farms and villages.

We stayed in the little hotel for a few weeks. It was now the middle of April and I had been gone since December. One day, Ah Loo told me that my parents had returned home and I could join them in a couple of days. Unfortunately, he also said that I couldn't take Borrow with me on the train. It was extremely difficult for me to give up the dog, but I also knew that my Father would never let me keep him at home. Sadly, Ah Loo and I now had to find a new home for Borrow. We remembered that on one of our walks through a small village in the hills, we had met a farm boy about my age. This boy, terribly envious that I had a dog, spent a lot of time petting Borrow. As we were leaving, we heard him pestering his mother to get him that dog. His mother patiently explained that this particular dog belonged to someone else, but one day she would get him a dog of his own. We both remembered the incident and agreed that Borrow would have a good home with that boy. Because we ventured out so often, however, it was difficult to remember exactly where the farmhouse was. It took us several tries, but we finally found it. Ah Loo talked to the peasant woman and she was happy to accept the dog. The boy, of course, was thrilled to have him. Somberly, I handed him Borrow's leash and brush. Tears were streaming down my face as Ah Loo took my hand and led me down the hill. I turned back to take one last look. Borrow was struggling against the leash, trying to follow me. I looked away quickly. At six, I had my first experience of real pain and sorrow. I had to part forever from someone I loved.

Chapter Twenty-two

Two days later, Ah Loo and I took the train back to Shanghai. When we arrived, a man was waiting for us on the platform whom Ah Loo introduced as "Tzou." We walked out of the station with Tzou, and Ah Loo said to me, "I want to take you to a nice restaurant for our last dinner together. I've really enjoyed having you with me this past four and a half months."

Ah Loo was the only one who had been with me from the first day to the last, and I thought he was a very sweet man. I had gotten used to his stuttering by now, and I no longer laughed at him.

We went to a restaurant called The Golden Gate and had a very nice early dinner. During dinner, Ah Loo and Tzou carried on a conversation, Tzou asking Ah Loo about different people. They seemed to be catching up on acquaintances who were familiar to both of them. Among the people I heard them talk about was my mother's second half brother, but I didn't give it much thought at the time.

After dinner, as we stood outside the restaurant, Ah Loo said to me, "Well, this is good-bye for us." I was astonished. I assumed he would take me home to my parents, rather than send me off with this stranger. I begged him to come home with me.

"I don't think your parents would like to see me," he said.

"I know they'll like you. They love friends," I argued. "And you are my friend."

"You're a big boy now. You shouldn't be afraid of going with Tzou. He'll take you home."

Ah Loo hugged me and kissed me on the cheek before putting me on Tzou's lap in a rickshaw. As I headed for home, he stood on the street and waved good-bye. I had developed a genuine fondness for Ah Loo, Godfather and my favorite playmate, Ah Fong. As a child, I could sense whether affection was real or phony. I knew these men all honestly loved me, and that Godfather would have liked to keep me as a son if circumstances had been different. As Tzou and I sat silently in the rickshaw, I wondered whether I would ever see any of them again.

When our rickshaw pulled up in front of my home, I jumped out before it even came to a stop and ran in the open back door. There was a lot of commotion in the kitchen. The cook was bustling around behind a cloud of steam from pots of cooking food. Mamma Chang was sitting on a bench cleaning vegetables. Running up to her, I said, "It looks like we're having a dinner party tonight. Great!"

She looked at me with her mouth open. Seconds passed but no sound came out, so I turned around and ran into the living room where about twenty or thirty men were congregating. My father was among them. As soon as I saw him, I stopped running. I walked up to him and addressed him properly, "Daddy!"

He just stared at me for what seemed like a long time. The other men also stared. No one uttered a word. Finally, my father said gently, "Your mother is waiting for you upstairs. Why don't you go up and see her?"

Relieved to hear this dismissal, I left the room and ran up the stairs into my parents' bedroom, which was filled with ladies. My mother was sitting on the edge of her bed. She later told me that her legs were so weak from fear that there was no way she could have stood to greet me. She feared that I had been tied-up and mistreated. She imagined that I would be emaciated and had my head shaved. I walked up to her and addressed her, "Mommy!"

With tears rolling down her cheeks, she reached out and held my shoulders in her hands. She pulled me to her and began to sob.

When she started crying, I began to cry also. As she held me and both of us cried, her friends crowded around and said to her, "Ada, please don't cry. He is home now and you should be happy. The sad days are over."

Mother nodded in agreement and dried her tears. She pulled away, looking me over, feeling my arms and my hands. In a surprised tone, she said, "You look so well. You are much taller and so healthy." With my four and a half months of fresh air and daily walks, I had a red glow in my cheeks and was much more robust than before. Everyone marveled at how great I looked in my new spring clothes.

After the initial excitement, my mother and her friends began asking me about my life during the past few months. With my newly acquired confidence and ability to converse with adults, I started telling them my story. I described my dog, books, toys, Godfather, Ah Fong, and did a very comical imitation of Ah Loo stuttering. I told them about the wedding I attended at the Hangchow Hotel. Mother gasped—she had been invited to that very wedding but because she was so upset that I was gone she didn't go to it. Suddenly, she looked at me,

"Didn't you know that you were kidnapped?"

"Kidnapped?" I was shocked. "But Godfather really loved me. Are you sure he was a kidnapper?"

"Yes, we paid a huge ransom for your return."

"But, they really truly liked me. Ah Loo even treated me to a good dinner before sending me home. He and Tzou acted like they were old friends. They talked about everyone they knew, even your half-brother."

Mother immediately sent a servant downstairs to see where Tzou was. During the commotion and excitement over my return, all the attention had been on me. No one noticed whether or not Tzou even entered the house behind me. Of course, he was nowhere to be found and was never seen again.

Chapter Twenty-three

The day I was kidnapped, Ada tried to stay calm and console Mamma Chang. She reasoned that all the kidnappers wanted was money and, if the ransom was paid, I would be returned in a few days. Father immediately called a poker buddy of his, the police commissioner for the newly established Chinese police force in Shanghai. A large group of police and detectives were mobilized, and they made a massive search for me, concentrating their efforts in and around Shanghai. By the time the detectives staked out the train station, however, I was already in another city. During the war years, cooperation between law enforcement units of different cities had totally broken down, so it was fruitless to expand the search very far beyond Shanghai's borders.

As the days turned into weeks and the police had nothing to report, Mother began to panic. She and Father were puzzled that the kidnappers had not come forth to make contact with the family as kidnappers almost always do. Distraught, she couldn't concentrate on her favorite game of Mahjong or participate in any of her usual social activities. She was no longer able to sleep at night. Even when she dozed off momentarily, she would wake up crying. Father didn't know what more he could do to find me or how to console Mother in this terrible situation. Fortunately, Aunt Jill decided to move into the townhouse to provide the support Ada needed. She slept on a cot in the same room as my parents and, every time Ada woke up crying, Jill would also get up, listen to my mother and talk to her, trying to calm her down. She would prepare hot towels with which Ada could wipe her face and hot tea to help soothe her. Eventually, Ada would calm down and again try to sleep. This would happen several times a night, every night. Jill stayed with Ada for the entire time I was gone and after my return, Ada told me how wonderful Aunt Jill had been through the ordeal. I should never forget her devotion and should treat her like a mother, with the same respect I showed to my natural mother. Later, Aunt Jill became my Godmother.

Jill insisted on daily activities outside the house, hoping to provide Ada with some distraction during daylight hours. In the mornings they always took shopping trips to various department stores. Ada had very little desire to buy anything, but it was a form of diversion. In the afternoons, they usually went to a new form of popular entertainment—storytelling. Each program would have four or five half-hour storytelling sessions, with a different storyteller and a different story in each session, and each continuing on the next day, like a soap opera. The storytellers were very well-trained actors who told the tales in riveting ways, acting out each character. Many ladies became very serious fans, and would not dream of missing a day. The plots developed so slowly, however, that you could still follow them if you missed a few sessions. The stories would stop each day at a suspenseful moment, to lure the audience back the next day. Ada and Jill attended regularly, like other devoted fans, but Ada could barely concentrate on the development of the stories.

When evenings came, Ada always fell into a deep depression. She stopped all of her social activities, even her favorite Mahjong game and the Peking Opera. Not brought up with any specific religion, Ada only knew to pray to heaven in a time of desperation. Late at night, she would kneel in the courtyard and pray for two or three hours and these prayer sessions soon turned into a nightly vigil. She would often collapse with stomach spasms from kneeling so long. When that happened, Zee, Jill and Mamma Chang would have to help her into the house. The disappearance of her only son was affecting Ada physically, as well as emotionally.

As the time I was away extended to two months, most of my parents' friends and relatives believed that I would never be found again, but Ada refused to give up hope. Every day, she would clean my cup, toothbrush and comb, and rearrange my towels in the bathroom. Everyone pitied her unrealistic hope for her little boy's return.

Ada and Zee finally convinced the police commissioner to call off the search. Word was out on the street that my parents would pay whatever ransom was requested for their son's safe return. Anyone who came forward to negotiate would be free from police harassment. Soon phone calls started coming in. Most of them, however, were from people trying to swindle cash from Ada and Zee. These callers claimed to have a connection to the kidnappers, and, if they were given some money first, would arrange the actual contact. Zee never fell for these scams. One of the calls did sound believable, however, so Ada and Zee agreed to meet the caller at a snack shop in a working-class neighborhood. The man claimed he knew who my kidnappers were. His story was convincing, but Zee insisted that no money would be paid until he saw proof of my actual existence. The man asked what kind of proof would be satisfactory. Ada said that she wanted a recent photograph of me taken with my hand at my forehead, as though I were saluting. The man agreed, but asked for a photo of me to be certain that the boy he had in mind was really me. A week later this man claimed that he had the picture Ada wanted. Ada and Zee met with him again. When they looked at the picture, they knew it was another hoax. It was the same photo Ada had given him the week before, except my clothes were retouched—changed from an white open collar shirt to a black Chinese Mandarin collar. My eyebrows had been thickened and looked bushy. Freakiest of all, a hand of an adult person had been superimposed on my forehead in a salutary position. Ada, overcome with disappointment, burst into tears when she saw the photograph. Zee rushed her out of the place, and she sobbed all the way home.

By late March, my parents still had no clue as to my whereabouts. One morning Jill and Ada were on their regular department store rounds when a man came up to Ada and said, "Hello! Do you remember me?"

Ada took a long look at the man and finally it came to her. "Yes, you were in my high school class in Wusi," she said. "But, forgive me, I can't recall your name."

"My name is Tzou," he reminded her.

After some niceties, Ada told him that she was married now and lived in Bubbling Well Villa. Offhandedly, she asked him to visit if he happened to be in the neighborhood, and gave him the house number.

The next day, after lunch, Tzou dropped in without notice. Zee was taking a nap, so Ada and Jill chatted with him in the living room over a cup of tea. He mentioned that he still lived in Wusi but came to Shanghai often, on business. He spoke about his wife and child and then asked, "Do you have any children, Ada?"

With that question, tears began to gush down Ada's cheeks. Jill immediately apologized for her friend and explained that Ada's son had been kidnapped. Tzou expressed sympathy and then mentioned that he knew someone involved with the underworld. Perhaps he could find some kind of a lead. Desperate, Ada begged him to look into the matter. She was at her wit's end. She told him that the police were completely removed from the case and she would guarantee the safety of anyone who made contact. Her only goal was the return of her son and she and Zee were willing to pay for that. As Tzou was leaving, he said that he didn't know if his connection was the right place to make an inquiry, but he would definitely try.

A few days later, on a Sunday morning, a servant announced that a gentleman was downstairs. He had asked to see Ada and Zee, but would not give his name. My parents and Jill looked at each other. In an instant the same thought went through all their minds:

"This could be the man we've been waiting for!"

They rushed downstairs to the living room and found a very well dressed man sitting on the sofa. He came straight to the point. "I have your child."

"How do we know?" Zee asked. "And, what kind of condition is the child in?"

"He is being very well taken care of and is in excellent condition. Name the kind of proof you want and I'll furnish it."

Ada jumped in, "I want a recent photograph, and a letter to me, written by the child himself."

The man stood up, and said, "O.K., I'll keep in touch." Then he left.

A week later, in early April, Mamma Chang rushed into the bedroom and whispered excitedly that the man was back. Ada and Zee hurried into the living room. The man handed Ada the letter written by me. She read it and said, "This couldn't be written by him. The handwriting is too good." Then, the man pulled out two 8 x 10 photos and showed them to her. Both Zee and Ada realized that this was the Real McCoy. The last question was the price.

"Two hundred large yellow fish," the man said flatly.

In China then, people called gold bars "yellow fish." A large yellow fish, about the size of a large flat cigar, weighed ten taels. A small yellow fish weighed one tael. During times of inflation, people often kept gold bars instead of cash. The ransom requested, two hundred large yellow fish, meant two thousand taels of pure gold. Zee was shocked by the high price and wondered how he could ever raise that much cash.

"I really like the child," the man said as he stood up. "It's O.K. if you don't want to pay the price. I'll be happy to keep him as my son."

Ada panicked and blurted out, "We'll pay, we'll pay!"

"I'll need some time to raise that kind of money," Zee quickly injected.

"I'll give you fifteen days. If you don't have the money ready by then, I won't make another contact with you again. I'll just keep the boy." With that, he left.

Zee did not have nearly that much cash and had to borrow it. On the fifteenth day, the man called on the phone. He demanded that the money be delivered two days before I would be returned. Also, he insisted that he approve of the person who was to both drop off the money, and pick me up two days later. Jill volunteered, but the man rejected her. My parents made several other suggestions, but he rejected them all. Finally, he gave Zee three more days to come up with someone who was acceptable to him.

A day later, Tzou came to visit again. Ada asked him if he was willing to be the person making the exchange. Tzou acted excited about the progress on the deal for my return, and agreed to take responsibility for the exchange. The kidnapper called two days later. To Ada's surprise and relief, he accepted Tzou as the "go-between man." On schedule, Tzou picked up the case of money and, according to what he told my parents, delivered it to some alley. Two days later Tzou reported that he was to pick me up from another alley. Of course, he was at the train station waiting for me and Ah Loo and then dined with us before I parted company with Ah Loo. After he took me home, he disappeared. When it finally dawned on my parents that Tzou was working with the kidnappers, he was long gone.

Chapter Twenty-four

When I returned home in late April of 1942, everyone noticed the change in me. Mamma Chang giggled, "He talks and acts like a little adult man."

I had picked up a lot of macho mannerisms and speech patterns from being with adult men for four and a half months. After I returned, however, it wasn't long before I slipped back into my shy mannerisms and hardly audible way of talking around grown-ups.

My parents were so paranoid after the kidnapping that I wasn't allowed out of the house without at least three or four adults accompanying me. I felt like a prisoner under house arrest. The wrought iron gates to the courtyard, which led to the front door of the house, were permanently locked and everyone had to use the back door next to the garage. The garage had been converted into a kitchen because the original kitchen was too cramped. Since the cook and other servants were always in the kitchen, no one could enter or leave the house without being seen by the kitchen staff. I could only play in the courtyard, in front of the house, where the eight-foot-high brick wall and permanently locked wrought iron gates protected me. At the top of the brick wall, broken glass shards were embedded in the cement. To insure additional privacy, my father had a workman cover the wrought iron gates with sheet metal so no one could see into the courtyard. I soon learned to use the sheet metal-wrapped gates as blackboards. With chalk, I would spend endless hours drawing animals, trees and flowers on the flat gray metal.

A tutor came to the house from eight-thirty a.m. to noon Mondays through Saturdays to help me with my studies. Since Ivy was in school every day, I was alone each afternoon when the tutor left.

Father came home from his office in the financial district for lunch, and I had to sit properly at the lunch table with him and mother. From the habit I developed during my kidnapping, I sometimes would launch into a conversation with Mother. Father would endure my chatting for a few minutes, and then would say, "Why don't you eat your lunch." That was his way of saying that I was talking too much. I would immediately stop and turn my attention back to my food.

Following lunch, Father routinely took a nap. After he awoke, he had early tea and then left to make rounds at his factory in the industrial area around four p.m. Mother usually stayed in bed until Father arrived for lunch, unless she and Jill planned to make a trip to the department stores, or had a morning lesson with their opera teacher. Ivy would rather have her lunch delivered to her school so she could eat with her friends. Like me, she felt that lunch with Father was too confining.

Aunt Jill was a regular at the lunch table, and there were often other guests as well. When the adults were conversing I didn't say a word, unless a question was directed at me. After lunch, while Father was napping, Mother would start her make-up and dressing program. She and Jill usually left for their Mahjong game or other activities around three, when Father was having his tea. After Father made his rounds at his factory, he would then be off to play cards with his poker buddies.

I couldn't make any noise in the house after lunch because both my parents were home. Mamma Chang was usually on her lunch break so, to pass the time, I would visit Mrs. Upstairs, my last remaining Grandmother, in her bedroom on the third floor. In her seventies now, she had her personal maid serve all her meals to her in her room. After she ate she would often get a stomach ache, so some of the relatives suggested that she use opium to relieve her pain. She tried it a few times, and it worked like a charm. Since it was perfectly legal to smoke opium at the time, Zee purchased a very fancy polished rosewood tray for Mrs. Upstairs to use. It had a beautiful little oil lamp with a dome-shaped glass shade resembling an igloo and a bamboo pipe with an ivory mouth piece and onion-shaped bowl. Her smoking paraphernalia also included many small silver boxes, 8" long silver needles and paddles looking like miniature long-handled Ping-Pong paddles. When I visited her in the early afternoon, she was usually lying in her bed, in the middle of her smoking session. I would pull up a stool and watch the entire ritual. I loved the pungent aroma which filled the room. Her maid was on her lunch break so the two of us chatted leisurely by ourselves. Often, I would get her to tell me stories from old Chinese folklore. I particularly liked "The Fox Spirit," a fairy-tale about a fox who had a special spirit, enabling it to turn into a beautiful woman.

After a while, I convinced Mrs. Upstairs to let me prepare her opium pipe. I had watched her countless times so I knew exactly how to dip the needle into the opium syrup, then heat it over the flame and roll it on the paddle. By repeating this process, you built up the size of the opium on the needle. When it was the size of a raisin, it was ready to be mounted on top of the onion bowl. Once it was atop the bowl, it was ready to be smoked above the open flame. I became so efficient in preparing Mrs. Upstairs' pipes that she laughed and said one day, "I bet your mother couldn't do this as well." She was right.

Chapter Twenty-five

In the late summer of 1942, I sensed something unusual around the house. The adults were all talking in hushed tones as though a secret was in the air. I had learned at an early age not to ask questions about grown-up affairs but I usually got the scoop by patiently putting together bits and pieces of conversations I overheard, particularly the servants' gossip. Through my detective work this time, I finally learned that Uncle Chi had gotten a dance hall girl pregnant. He was a regular patron of night spots where pretty girls were provided as dance partners. Twenty-nine, handsome, wealthy and a bonafide bachelor, he was of great interest to all the girls at the clubs. Among them, a girl named "Fragrance" was particularly bright and pretty. She soon managed to make herself the primary object of Chi's attention and the others were washed away in her wake. Afraid to lose him, she used the only way she knew how to keep him—she got pregnant.

Only eighteen and with just a fourth-grade education, she was not the kind of girl Chi intended to marry. What would people say if he married an uneducated dance hall girl? Her family, however, was making serious threats, and worse, she had threatened to take her life if he refused to marry her. Chi sat up night after night trying to find a solution to his dilemma. Zee and Ada sat up with him many nights. Zee offered to pay off the girl and her family with a sizable amount of cash, plus the cost of an abortion. Chi, however, was afraid that Fragrance would truly commit suicide. Ada tried to help Chi come to a decision. She told him that both she and Zee were quite open-minded and would not resent having a sister-in-law who had been a dance hall girl. Education and background are less important than the character of the girl—what counts is that she is a nice girl. Ada also advised Chi not to worry about what other people would say. Finally, Chi decided to marry Fragrance. Zee and Ada paid a visit to her home and found Fragrance to be, in fact, a very nice girl. They felt even more sympathetic to her when they heard the story of her sad life. Her father had died several years ago and her traditional mother, with bound feet, had no skills with which to make a living. Fragrance had a homely older sister and two younger brothers, and she and her sister had to quit school so the boys could continue their education. Fragrance was pretty so she was the only one who could earn enough money to support the family, albeit very meagerly. She had been working in the dance hall since she was fifteen.

A small, hastily-planned wedding was held in the private dining room of a restaurant. Only twelve people attended, including the bride and groom. Ivy and I were among the guests. The bride wore a peach colored Chinese style sheath for the brief ceremony, which clung a little too tightly to her six-months-pregnant body.

After the ceremony, the wedding party had dinner in the same private dining room. Ada left the dinner a little early to check the preparations for a small reception at home in honor of the bride's arrival. To everyone's surprise, Mrs. Upstairs had refused to attend the wedding. With her own bordello background, no one could understand her objection to the marriage. She never said whether she was upset because Fragrance had been a dance hall girl, or because of her pregnancy. Once home, Ada dashed up to the third floor and pleaded with Mrs. Upstairs to at least come down to toast the newlyweds, finally managing to coax her down to the living room. Soon after, a maid announced that the bride and groom had arrived. Mrs. Upstairs stood up tensely and tried to retreat to the back of the crowd as the newlyweds entered the room. Chi spotted her and immediately gave Fragrance's hand a quick tug.

They swiftly walked over and knelt down in front of Mrs. Upstairs. Confronted with this formal introduction, Mrs. Upstairs was forced to come forward and ask them to rise, but it was clear to all that she took no pleasure in doing so. Nothing that remotely resembled a smile graced her lips.

That night, Fragrance settled into the third floor bedroom with Chi. She brought her entire worldly belongings with her, in two small suitcases. Three months later, at the China Convalescent Hospital, she gave birth to a healthy baby boy. Into the more and more crowded townhouse, Fragrance and Chi brought a wet nurse, who occupied the small bedroom on the third floor. Zee then hired a male chef who had worked for the family at the Changchow compound. This temperamental chef insisted on having a male assistant to do his prep work, pump the bellows and carry heavy grocery bags home from the market. With all the rooms taken, these two cooks had to sleep in sleeping bags in the living room.

Ada soon took on a new project—the remaking of Fragrance. She took her shopping and taught her to dress elegantly. She showed her how to apply her make up with a lighter touch and a new subdued effect, and schooled her in all the different social graces. When Fragrance was first introduced into Ada's social circle, she spoke very little, not wanting to display her ignorance. She carefully observed Ada at these functions and, since she was young and eager to learn, acquired the mannerisms and social graces of an upper-class lady in no time. When she first married, Fragrance was just a teenager and often had bouts of acne. After the birth of her child, however, her skin cleared up completely and her figure ripened. With the help of more subtle make-up and a new wardrobe, she matured into a stunning beauty. She also became an expert Mahjong player. Naturally, she picked up Ada's schedule as well. She stayed in bed until lunch time, except for shopping days at the department stores, or Peking Opera singing lessons.

Most days, the two women would spend a minimum of two hours on their make-up and dressing routine after lunch. Then Jill would arrive and off they would all go for the balance of the day and evening. Ada's and Fragrance's chic styles were soon becoming the talk of the neighborhood. At three o'clock every afternoon, neighbors would station themselves at their windows or doorways in order to catch a glimpse of the two fashion plates and check out their latest outfits.

Chi spent his afternoons at the race track, and the evenings at poker games with his cronies, a younger crowd than Zee's group.

From the life style of my parents and uncle and aunt, it was hard to believe there was a war going on.

Chapter Twenty-six ━━━━━━━

After returning from my kidnapping experience, I was house bound for over a year—from April 1942 to August 1943. Compared to life with my kidnappers, it was a very boring sixteen-month period for me. I understood, of course, why I had to be watched at all times, and went along with the program. I was too important and my parents loved me too much to take chances on losing me again. They had already paid dearly for my return.

In September, 1943, I was finally enrolled in a new private school for boys, much farther away from home than the previous school I had attended. Mamma Chang took me to school in a rickshaw every day so I wouldn't have to walk on the street. Despite that, I was relieved to be back in school and no longer house bound.

In my previous school I had been too shy to talk to the other students and hadn't made friends. I had always clung to Mamma Chang during recess and refused to play with others even when they asked me. In the past year, however, my personality had changed a great deal, and I was anticipating a more exciting life on this new campus. For my first day in the fourth grade, I arrived at the new school, which had several buildings, a large playground and a soccer field. The tallest boy in my class, who was very gregarious, befriended me that day and we soon became best friends. In the same school since kindergarten, he was familiar with everything, and I totally relied on him. He introduced me to his soccer-playing buddies and taught me the rules of the game. I was anxious to be accepted by his elite group of friends so, with all the energy I had, I threw myself into playing soccer. I played during the ten-minute recess, gobbled down a few bites of lunch at midday and started playing again. After school, Mamma Chang had to bodily drag me off the field because my tutor was waiting at home. By November, I had become very thin and my complexion had turned dark from so much exposure to the sun. In my family's social circle, it was definitely not fashionable to be tan. Displeased with my appearance, Mother said that I looked like a farmer's son rather than a little gentleman from a nice family. She also warned that I was too thin. I argued, however, that as long as I was healthy, it didn't matter whether I was fat or thin. Mother seemed to realize that I was growing older and becoming more independent. She tried to curb her tendency to be overly protective and stopped nagging me about my weight and my tan.

When winter vacation came, I was home for three weeks. Mamma Chang remarked that I looked a lot better since I had stopped playing soccer—my sunken cheeks were filling out, and my forehead no longer looked like it had been charred. As soon as I was back in school, however, I resumed my fanatical approach to soccer. By March, I collapsed with a fever. Uncle Chou was summoned and, since he specialized in orthopedics, he brought with him a pediatrician who was a Yale graduate, Dr. Foo. They discussed my illness with each other in English so people in the household wouldn't misinterpret their analysis. My parents looked at them with admiration but, of course, didn't understand a word they were saying. That might have been the moment when Mother first decided that I should be a doctor when I grew up.

After a few days, I was officially diagnosed with pleurisy. Mother went into a panic, having heard that pleurisy patients have to have their ribs removed. Uncle Chou assured her that I was still in a very early stage of the disease and surgery would not be necessary. All I needed was rest and nutritious food. He also warned Mother that because of both my lowered immunity and the bad air pollution in the city, I was at risk for tuberculosis, a common disease among the poor in China.

Mother immediately insisted that everyone in the household have chest x-rays taken. The x-rays revealed that the chef had tuberculosis and he was immediately dismissed. Mother contacted Mr. and Mrs. Nu, whose mansion on the edge of the city adjacent to a vast farmland had been my first home in Shanghai. Without hesitation, Mrs. Nu agreed to rent out part of her house for my convalescence.

My parents hired Uncle Chou's widowed sister, a retired grade school teacher, to be my governess during the recuperation period. In May of 1944, my new governess, Mamma Chang and I packed up and moved to the Nu's suburban home.

Chapter Twenty-seven

At the Nu residence, we occupied a very large sunny bedroom on the second floor, with an enormous bay window. A pair of twin beds were set up for me and my governess, and Mamma Chang slept on the sofa in the bay window area. In the middle of the room there was a large square table where I ate and did my schoolwork. A small room on the first floor next to the breezeway was converted to a kitchen for Mamma Chang to prepare meals for the three of us. She cooked a variety of mouthwatering dishes to increase my appetite and fed me an abundance of nutritious food four times a day. I soon developed into a hearty eater and have stayed one throughout my life.

Every two or three afternoons, on her way to her Mahjong game, Mother would visit me, usually bringing me cakes and ice cream as treats. As time went on, she cut down her visits to every Sunday afternoon. Father never visited me, but I accepted that and never really missed him.

In the beginning, I rested much of the time. My governess didn't want to put pressure on me so my studies were extremely light. After three months, however, I was my robust self again and was allowed to take daily walks in the garden with my governess. My morning study load also increased dramatically but, after lunch,

I still had to take my mandatory daily nap. My favorite time of the day was after my four o' clock meal, when the Nu's children returned from school. I really enjoyed the companionship of those kids, who would congregate in my room and play with me until dinner time. I had gradually become a very outgoing person and enjoyed being the center of attention. With much embellishment and animation, I would entertain the other children, acting out the stories I had read in the morning.

In September, Uncle Chou said I was cured but cautioned me against overexertion. Though Mother retained my room at the Nu residence, I often went home for a two or three-day visit. To my surprise, after my long absence, my bedroom had been converted into a Mahjong room and my bed had been removed to make room for the game tables. When I visited, my parents pushed their twin beds together so I could sleep in between them. All the fashionable couples in Shanghai at that time slept in separate twin beds, influenced by what they saw in the 1930s Hollywood movies. Many furniture stores in the city didn't even sell double beds. I enjoyed these visits, and particularly sleeping in my parents' room. The lights would stay on each night until they returned home from their social activities in the wee hours of the morning. Occasionally, I would wake up and they would let me join them for their midnight supper. Mother would tuck a little money under my pillow if she won at her Mahjong game. Some nights, she even took me with her to the Peking Opera. I was small enough to share her seat without having to have a separate ticket. Since I was not required to study on these visits, they were like holidays for me.

Around that time, several super deluxe gambling casinos opened up in Shanghai which attracted the chic "in" crowd. For a change of pace, Zee and Chi went out a few times to these new casinos with their wives. It was very unusual to see the four of them going out together. To mingle in public at the casinos, Ada and Fragrance made sure they dressed up in an exceptionally glamorous manner. When they arrived at a club, Zee and Chi would hit the poker or blackjack tables, while Ada and Fragrance spent their time at the roulette wheel. These casino nights, however, were but a passing fancy and the novelty soon wore off. Ada and Fragrance returned to their friends and their favorite game of

Mahjong, and Zee and Chi went back to their respective poker buddies.

In November, I moved back home for good. My bed was returned to my bedroom but Mother still used my room for Mahjong when the game rotated to our house. I loved drifting off to sleep amidst the sounds of the banging Mahjong tiles and the laughing and talking of the women. Thanks to that experience, I learned to sleep through any kind of disturbance, throughout my life.

My governess was discharged because we didn't have enough space in the townhouse for another live-in. A new tutor was hired, who came every morning, Monday through Friday. I rarely saw Ivy except at dinner time. Soon to be fifteen, she was very popular and had a large group of friends from school. She would much rather go out with her friends than be pestered by her little brother at home. She was now enrolled in a middle school with a very high tuition but a lax academic program—the type of institution which catered to rich kids who liked to party. Since she was a girl, our parents didn't harp on her about her studies. She wasn't even punished when her grades were so bad that she had to repeat the same grade. Older than her classmates, she became their leader in all kinds of activities, from planning parties to playing hooky. I envied her fun-filled life. All I could look forward to was the Sunday afternoon movie with Mother, followed by afternoon tea at one of those European coffee shops.

Chapter Twenty-eight ───────

One Sunday afternoon, I went to a movie with Mother as usual. Afterwards, we stopped by "D.D.'s" for a snack. When we walked in, a tall and handsome man joined us, whom Mother introduced as "Uncle Frank." He was in his mid-30s and wore a nice three-piece suit. There were several slot machines in the corner of this restaurant which, to play, required special tokens. Uncle Frank handed me two handfuls of tokens to keep me busy and away from the table while he and mother talked. When I lost all my tokens, I returned to the table for an ice cream soda and pastries. Then we said good-bye to Uncle Frank and left. Mother and I walked the three blocks home and she casually told me I was not to mention meeting Uncle Frank to anyone at home. I gladly went along with her request and thought nothing more about it.

The following Sunday afternoon, Mother took me to an afternoon tea dance at an exclusive night club. The club, called The Seventh Heaven, no doubt from the Janet Gaynor movie with the same title, was on the seventh floor of a high-rise building. When we entered, Uncle Frank, who was waiting at a table, stood up to greet us. We sat at his table and ordered ice cream, sandwiches and tea. Mother and Uncle Frank went out to the dance floor to dance a couple of times, leaving me at the table with all the goodies. We stayed about an hour and a half, then Mother and I said good-bye to Uncle Frank. We took a pedicab home, which had recently replaced most rickshaws. They carried two passengers, took less energy and were much faster than the rickshaw, which carried only one adult passenger.

One day when Mother and I were alone, she asked, "Would you like to visit Uncle Frank sometime? He is very fond of you."

"Sure, I'd love to visit him," I said. "Are you going to take me?"

"No, I won't be seeing him again. Auntie Hwa will take you, if you have no objection." Auntie Hwa had been a long and loyal friend of my mother's. She still came to visit every Sunday, her day off from her hospital job. She also gave Ivy and me shots and vaccines when necessary. Though her short hair, manly attire and stocky build made her rather unattractive, we all liked her and were accustomed to her eccentricity.

Auntie Hwa now came regularly on Sunday afternoons to take me to Uncle Frank's apartment, explaining to anyone who might ask that she was taking me to the park. Uncle Frank was always waiting for me at his beautiful apartment. It was decorated in a masculine English style and had the first wall-to-wall carpeted room I had ever seen. He had many toys, books and games for me to play with, and gave me new presents each time I visited. I couldn't bring anything home with me, however, so eventually, he had to empty an entire closet to accommodate all my playthings. Of course, I managed to drag everything out of that closet each time I was there. Sitting on his carpeted floor, Uncle Frank played games and read books to me. I had never had any affection from my father at home, and Uncle Frank, like Godfather and my other kidnappers had been, quickly became a substitute father to me. I treasured the two hours I spent with him every Sunday afternoon. I realized, even though Mother had never said another word, that this was a secret between us and didn't mention the visits to anyone at home.

Winter was upon us, and Mrs. Upstairs' health was failing. She was diagnosed with liver cancer and had wasted away so much that she looked like a skeleton. Opium no longer alleviated her excruciating pain so morphine was prescribed for her. Eventually, she became totally incoherent and Ivy and I were not allowed to enter her room. One Sunday, while I was away at my weekly visit with Uncle Frank, Mrs. Upstairs passed away. If she were their natural mother, my Father and Uncle could not have treated her better. Ada and Fragrance also showed Mrs. Upstairs the utmost respect. Still, I often wondered whether she had been happy at all in her life, or if she had wished for something different.

A three-day funeral was held in a Buddhist temple, one of the few buildings in Shanghai with a Chinese design and architectural style. Massive lacquered columns supported the temple's traditional heavily tiled roof with curved-up corners. A large courtyard, which led up to the main hall, was just inside the entrance gate. In the middle of the main hall, a life-sized portrait of Mrs. Upstairs, in a gilded frame, was set up.

Surrounding the portrait were enough flowers to have filled several floral shops. In front of the portrait was a table, which served as an altar. It was covered with lit candles and incense sticks, and several kneeling pads were in front of it. White cotton curtains formed an enormous backdrop and, behind the curtains, Mrs. Upstairs' body was laid out in an open coffin. Three musicians were hired to play Chinese flutes and three peasant women were hired as criers. When a guest walked through the front gate, the musicians, who were stationed there, started their music. The flutes signaled the criers, who were sitting behind the curtains, to let loose with loud wails and mournful cries. The guest would pay his or her respects in front of the altar table by kneeling or bowing, depending on his or her relationship with the deceased. Then the music and crying would stop as the guest went behind the curtains to view the body. Finally, the guest would pay a short visit to the family members, who were waiting in a series of sitting rooms on each side of the main hall. Tea and snacks were always served in these rooms, and lunch and dinner were provided at the appropriate times. Guests arrived continuously on the first day and the music and wailing carried on nonstop. The musicians and the crying women had to take turns in order to get a break. By the third day, however, there were long periods during which no one arrived. I was amused at how the three women sat behind the curtains chit-chatting, sometimes laughing and joking, and as soon as the flute music signaled, they immediately covered their faces with large cotton hankies and let loose with their crescendo of mournful howling.

Members of the family wore traditional white cotton mourning robes over their clothes. The women also wore a white cotton flower in their hair as a sign of bereavement. Every day a ceremony was performed, which was supposed to help the deceased safely reach the other side. As incense smoke filled the temple, about fifty Buddhist monks and nuns would parade around in bright orange robes, chanting loudly and beating on huge wooden fish. Everything the late Mrs. Upstairs would need in the other world—clothes, shoes, money, gold bars, toy-sized houses, cars, a sedan chair, rickshaw, dolls that represented maids, cooks, as well as chauffeurs and rickshaw pullers—was made out of paper and then burned in a big fire at the end of each ceremony. The parting spirit, it was believed, would then receive these goods for use on the other side.

The second afternoon was the official time to close the coffin, and an even more elaborate ritual was carried out at that time. I thoroughly enjoyed the colors, sounds and smells that were part of the pageantry. Since only a few guests came after the first day, several Mahjong tables were set up in the side rooms, for everyone to pass the time. The burial took place on the fourth day.

Afterwards, at home, Mrs. Upstairs' portrait was placed in the middle of a temporary shrine in the living room. It remained there for three months.

One morning not long after the funeral, Mother went into the living room and closed the door behind her. After a while, a maid came out and told Mamma Chang that the Madam was alone, crying in the living room.

Mamma Chang asked me to go comfort my mother, who must be very sad over the loss of Mrs. Upstairs. I entered the living room. My mother was sitting on the kneeling pad in front of the shrine, sobbing uncontrollably. I went up to her and put my hand on her shoulder, but didn't know what to say. Mamma Chang came in with a cup of tea and a hot towel. She quickly set the tray down and exited, closing the door behind her. After a while, Mother stopped crying. I handed her the towel and she wiped her eyes, then sipped her tea in silence. After a long silence, she finally managed to speak to me. In a very low voice, she asked, "Do you remember Uncle Frank?"

"Of course," I replied. "I just visited him a week ago."

"He is dead!" she exclaimed. Shocked, I just stared at her with unbelieving eyes. I had grown close to him, much closer than I was to my own father. It was a devastating loss to me. Tears suddenly started welling up in my eyes. Mother gently pulled me into her arms and cradled me in her lap as she sat on the kneeling pad. As the tears flowed down my cheeks she quietly told me a story that no one else in our family knew. Uncle Frank was the man she had been in love with before she met and married my father. They had planned to marry, but one day he simply disappeared without a word. Mother was heartbroken. A few days before I first met him, she had run into him after these many years in a restaurant. He asked her to have tea with him at "D.D.'s" for old times' sake. She agreed. To demonstrate that she was indeed a happily married woman with a son and a family life, she brought me along. While I was playing the slot machines that day, Frank told her his story. In 1929, realizing that war with the Japanese was imminent, he felt compelled to serve his country. He signed up to do intelligence work for the Chinese government and was to be sent to England for training as a wartime secret agent. He knew that a family life would be totally out of the question and didn't want to waste Ada's life. Hoping that Ada would marry someone else and have a happy life, he just disappeared, without giving her any explanation. When Ada ran into him at the restaurant over a decade later, he was a well-trained agent working in occupied Shanghai. With his elegant manners and superior education, he had obtained a position in the puppet government set up by the Japanese—unbeknownst, of course, to the Japanese. Despite the absence of more than fifteen years, both he and Ada still had strong feelings for one another but they knew it would be wrong to continue seeing each other. When Frank met me, he felt that I was the son he was never able to have with Ada and, since he could not share his love with the woman he loved, he transferred his feelings to her most beloved son. Ada agreed to let him see me and that was how my Sunday afternoon visits began.

Frank's secret identity had recently been discovered by the Japanese intelligence network and they came to arrest him. Due to the well-documented cruelty and torture practiced by the Japanese, Chinese agents were trained to take their own lives if arrest was unavoidable. Frank took cyanide pills and died. As Mother told me this story, both of us sobbed for a long time. Mrs. Upstairs' recent death served as a good cover for our grief.

A few months later, Auntie Hwa brought Mother a small suitcase which contained a few of Uncle Frank's possessions. I immediately recognized a heavy gold ring which he always wore. Once, I had even asked him to take it off and let me play with it. There was a fancy engraving on the top and I asked him what it was. He showed me the three interlaced English letters—"A" "D" "A"—my mother's name in English.

Mother took the ring out of the suitcase and always kept it in her dressing table drawer. Many years later, when I graduated from college in America, Mother asked me if there was anything I would particularly like for my graduation. I asked for the man's gold ring in her dressing table drawer, with her name engraved on it. She was very surprised and also very pleased that I still remembered that ring. By then she was living in Hong Kong and the ring was still in Shanghai, which had become part of Communist China. She managed to smuggle it out of China during one of her visits to see my Father and sent it to me in Los Angeles. I'm still in possession of that ring today. It is one of my most treasured possessions.

After this experience, I became Mother's closest confidant. We rarely needed words to express our feelings.

Chapter Twenty-nine ───────

It was 1944 and Auntie Jill was in love. For the past year, she had been on a serious diet and had gradually controlled her overeating, while slimming down to a new svelte size. She no longer had acne breakouts so her complexion was remarkably improved and, though you would not call her beautiful, with her excellent taste in clothing, she was a smart looking woman indeed. Her new boyfriend, Yu, had inherited the largest shipping business in Asia from his father, as well as a ship building factory. When the Japanese occupied Shanghai, they commandeered his entire fleet for transporting military supplies around Southeast Asia. Though he was paid by the puppet government, he hated aiding the enemy. Unfortunately, he had no alternative other than to cooperate with them. Meanwhile, Yu's older sister was married to the Attorney General in Chiang Kai-Shek's government and she encouraged Yu to join them. He finally decided to cross the battle lines and do his part to aid the Nationalist government in Chungking. Naturally, Jill wanted to go with him.

The day they were leaving, Aunt Jill and Uncle Yu, dressed in tattered peasant clothes, came to our home to say their farewells. For Ada and Jill, such lifelong friends, it was a very sad day. Ada was worried about Jill's safety on the long and perilous journey.

Jill and Yu could only travel by train for part of the way and then had to take ox carts or go on foot for many miles through the mountain regions. With their strong love for each other, however, Jill and Yu were willing to face the danger, and either survive or perish together. Fortunately, they made it to Chunking. While there, Jill and Yu married.

Meanwhile, Uncle Chi, who refused to take financial advice from his brother Zee, had built up a sizable debt because of some bad investments he had made. He now wanted to divide the property he shared with Zee so he could do whatever he wanted with his money without Zee's interference. Also, neither Chi nor Fragrance liked getting their monthly allowances from Zee any more and wanted to manage their own money. Zee agreed and hired a lawyer to draw up an equitable division of the estate. Chi didn't want any part of Zee's New China Spinning Mills so, as compensation, he got a larger percentage of the Success Textiles stock. Of the real estate Zee had purchased, Chi chose the two larger houses instead of the four smaller houses because the larger ones were valued higher.

After the property was divided, Chi sold the two houses and some of his Success Textiles stocks to pay off his debts. He retained enough stock to live a comfortable life on his dividends, which he did, never working a day in his life.

In 1943 and 1944, Aunt Fragrance had two more children, a girl and a boy. Chi's family took over the entire third floor now that Mrs. Upstairs had passed away. They ran a separate household and hired their own cook, maids, nannies and wet nurses. Also, my father wanted his own private pedicab so he hired a driver to peddle it. This man had to sleep on the living room floor with several other male servants. It was difficult for my parents and Uncle Chi, who were used to ample space in my grandfather's estate, to live under these crowded conditions. Yet everyone seemed to manage without getting on each other's nerves.

Of course, our crowded conditions could never compare to the poverty and hardship experienced by so many in the city all around us, even in our neighborhood. The garage of the townhouse next door was rented to a tailor and his family. Every year, it seemed, the tailor's wife had another baby and they now had about seven children. The entire family slept in a small loft they had built in the garage. The ground floor was filled with tables where the tailor and his two helpers sewed. The wife cooked dinner on a portable stove on the sidewalk and the only running water they had was from a faucet on the outside of the garage.

Seeing how the tailor's family lived, I knew we didn't have anything to complain about. In fact, I probably had more money myself as a young boy than that entire family did, at least at the Chinese New Year—a very profitable time for me and for all of the children in our family. On New Year's Eve, Mother always prepared a "long life tray" of candies and nuts, one for Ivy and another for me. A tangerine with a sprig of cypress, the symbol of long life, would be placed on top of each heaping tray, and under the tangerine was a red envelope containing brand new uncirculated money. This "long life money" was a traditional gift from grown-ups to children during the New Year season. Since most of our friends and relatives were well-to-do, I always collected a large sum of cash from every adult. Dozens of kids visited our house on New Year's day—the one day of the year children were not to be disciplined. We all had plenty of cash in our pockets and bought lots of fireworks to set off on the street. Then we usually gambled with our money, tossing dice on the floor. After three days, however, Mother always took the cash I had left from the red envelopes I collected, explaining that a child should not carry such large sums of money in his pocket. She saved this money for my future, converting it to U.S. dollars to guard against inflation. If she had some extra cash on hand, she would add it to the pot. Mother told me that father would pay for my tuition and room and board when I went to a University abroad, but he might be tightfisted when it came to giving me pocket money. Thus it was never too early, she said, to start saving for my pocket money. By the beginning of 1945, I already had $2,000 U.S. dollars saved for my future.

Chapter Thirty

Not long after the New Year's festivities in early 1945, Ada began to suspect that Zee had a mistress. A few months earlier, Fragrance and Chi had just had a huge fight over the fact that Chi had stayed out all night on more than one occasion. He would say he had been playing cards all night but Fragrance didn't buy his story. She was sure that her handsome husband was having an affair. One afternoon, she followed Chi and saw him enter an apartment. She waited a few minutes, then rang the door bell. When a very pretty girl opened the door, Fragrance stepped up to her and slapped her hard across the face. The slap instigated a full-on fight between the two women. Hearing it, Chi rushed out. He pushed the girl back inside the apartment and slammed the door shut. He stood there on the doorstep glaring at Fragrance, then took her by the arm and pulled her into a pedicab. Neither of them wanted to continue the scene in public so they sat in silence during the ride home. As soon as they reached the house, Fragrance ran up to the third floor, with Chi in hot pursuit. Once in their room, all hell broke loose. Down below, we heard screaming and yelling, followed by sounds of crashing furniture and objects being smashed to pieces. They were having a major physical fight. The commotion awakened Zee from his nap. Ada was in the middle of her make-up routine. Years ago, she had plucked her eyebrows and they never grew back so each day she had to paint on her eyebrows. On this day, as she and Zee ran up to the third floor to be peacemakers, Ada only had one eyebrow painted and was a very comical sight. Looking at Ada, the fighting couple burst out laughing but, by now, the bedroom was completely trashed. Ada pulled Fragrance aside and advised her not to fight—she was sure to be on the losing end since Chi was so big and strong. Fragrance, nursing her bruised cheek and starting to cry, asked Ada what would she do if she was in the same situation.

"Oh, I would leave him, I guess," Ada quipped.

Fragrance knew, however, that she did not have the same clout with Chi that Ada possessed with Zee. She worried that if she threatened to leave, it would be just what Chi wanted. She also dreaded more than anything the thought of returning to the life of hardship she had lived before her marriage. Chi's position was that he was entitled to have a "mistress outside," as a woman with whom a married man was having an affair was called in those days. Before China became a republic, wealthy men like Chi's and Zee's father routinely had many wives. When the law changed, prohibiting polygamy, the customs of men like them didn't change as easily, and many households still had more than one wife. Chi actually thought he was being respectful of Fragrance for not bringing his mistress into the household. After days of talking it over, Chi's hard line attitude finally won out. Fragrance had to accept sharing her husband with another woman. That did not stop her, however, from putting up a fight now and then, especially when Chi stayed out all night.

One day, Fragrance remarked to Ada, "Men are all alike. You better pay close attention to Zee. Someday, even he might play around."

Ada just shrugged it off. Zee had never stayed out all night, and Ada knew where he was at all times. His nightly poker games were always at his friends' homes, and all the players were married men. Wives were never invited to these games because the men felt constrained with them around, believing that if their nagging wives were there, they were more likely to lose money. The wives were happy to stay away—not wanting to take the blame for their husbands' losing streaks. At some point, however, the men decided they did want some "lady luck" on hand to help them win, so each night they hired eight call girls to come to the game, one for each of the players. The girls' duties were to pour drinks, massage the man's shoulders and neck, or hold his hand for good luck. Most of the wives, including Ada, knew about this arrangement. When the game rotated to our house, Ivy and I would often hang on the stair railing in order to look through the transom window above the living room door and get a peek at the call girls. Most of them were very pretty, fashionable young women, though usually overdressed, and with very heavy make-up. One of the wives didn't know about the call girls and when she found out, barged into the poker game unannounced.

A call girl was sitting next to her husband, holding his hand, and the wife marched up to the two of them, slapped the call girl across the face and dragged her husband out of the room. That was the poor man's last poker night. The rest of the men didn't want him around anymore because they felt he had a "shrew" for a wife. Zee came home and told Ada about this incident, which he thought was quite comical. The women in Ada's circle also criticized the wife for creating such a scene. It was considered very low class.

As time went on, Ada began to hear more and more about successful businessmen in their social circle having mistresses outside and decided she should pay closer attention to Zee's schedule and daily whereabouts. The easiest way for Ada to gain information was to interrogate Zee's full-time pedicab driver. One day when Zee was at the office, she summoned his driver upstairs to answer some questions. He was petrified. As Ada questioned him, he stuttered and stammered, the perfect example of a very bad liar.

Then, Ada bluffed, "I already know about the woman outside. All I want to know is her address. You better not lie to me if you want to stay employed here."

The man was totally taken in by Ada's bluff. In a breath he spilled out the address and also disclosed the existence of her two children, a three-year-old and one-year-old, both girls. This shocking discovery hit Ada like thunder crashing over her head. It was time for the man to leave to pick up Zee and bring him home for lunch. Ada warned him not to let Zee know about their conversation.

Ada waited for Zee's return. As soon as he entered the bedroom, she threw a radio at him. He ducked as it flew across the room and crashed onto the floor in a hundred pieces.

"What's the matter, dear?" Zee hurriedly asked, in a frightened tone, "What is the matter?"

Ada was so upset that she could hardly utter a word.

"Please, don't be angry," Zee kept saying. "Whatever it is, I assure you that we can solve the problem by talking it over."

Finally, she exploded. "You! You have a woman outside! She has two kids!" She repeated the last words, "TWO KIDS!"

Suddenly, Ada had trouble breathing and fainted dead away. Zee leaped forward and caught her before she hit the floor. Mamma Chang appeared and ushered Ivy and me away from the doorway where we had front-row seats after hearing the crash of the radio. The maids rushed to get a cold towel and hot tea for Ada. Zee applied acupressure to her, pushing on the spot between her nose and her upper lip. It was all very dramatic. After a few minutes, she started to come around. When she opened her eyes and saw Zee holding her in his arms, she jumped up and pushed him away.

"You really did it this time," she cried. "We're through!"

"Don't be upset, please don't be upset," Zee begged. "It's bad for your health. Everything can be resolved. I'll do anything you say. Anything!"

Ada sent a maid out to hail a pedicab. Zee put his hand on her arm and pleaded for her to stay. She spun around. Her eyes were big and round from rage. In a menacing tone she growled, "Don't you dare stop me." Zee meekly dropped his hand. She threw her black cashmere coat with a fluffy stone martin collar over her shoulders and briskly walked downstairs and out the door.

Chapter Thirty-one

After Ada stormed out of the house, Ivy and I sat silently at lunch with Father. Later that evening, Ada called Mamma Chang and instructed her to pack some suitcases and have them delivered to her younger sister Dan-Yee's home. Then, she spoke briefly with Ivy and me, making us promise to obey Mamma Chang and be respectful toward Father. We were both on Mother's side and were quite angry with Father, but she told us that Father had wronged her, not us.

Days went by. Zee couldn't convince Dan-Yee to tell him where Ada was hiding out. She had told Ivy and me that she was staying at her Aunt's, where she had first met Zee, but made us promise not to tell him where she was. She told us not to worry—if she decided to settle somewhere else she would take us with her. Father asked us if we knew where she was. We said we didn't know, of course, but he knew we did.

Finally, a lawyer called to inform Zee that Ada was suing for divorce. Zee panicked! He begged and pleaded with the lawyer, asking him not to go ahead with the divorce proceedings. If his beloved Ada would return home, Zee promised he would meet any of her demands. He simply couldn't live without her.

The lawyer came back to Zee with Ada's sole condition—he

had to get rid of the mistress. Since his children with the mistress were innocent victims, Ada was willing to raise them with Ivy and me.

Zee agreed to Ada's demand, but the mistress, whom everyone called "No. 8," refused to give up her children and asked for an outlandish amount of cash as a settlement. To pay it, Zee would have to liquidate some of his businesses. If that was what he needed to do in order for Ada to return home, however, he was more than happy to comply.

Philandering husbands were still very much accepted in Chinese society, while jealous wives were said to have "bad virtue." Ada was severely criticized by almost everyone in their social circle for asking for a divorce just because her husband had a mistress outside, a setup which was common among many successful businessmen. Ada's friends told her that people were talking behind her back and many accused her of trying to force her husband into bankruptcy. Everyone was shocked that she was so heartless. Other close friends advised Ada that it would be much cheaper to let Zee keep the mistress and simply give her a monthly allowance.

Ada felt pressured by all these opinions and wasn't sure what she should do. She decided to go to a fortune teller for guidance. From the way Ada was dressed, the fortune teller immediately recognized a high paying client. After a nice long chat, he figured out why she was there. When it was time for him to give her his words of wisdom, he told her that her family life had been too perfect. This perfect life might have caused the jealous Gods to cast bad luck on her or on her only child. To ward off their wrath, she needed to allow some imperfection in her life—such as another woman in her husband's life. This would break the spell cast upon her or her child. It was written in the book of her fate, he added, that her husband would always have outside affairs. If she got rid of one woman, another would soon take her place.

The session with the fortune teller was the final straw. Ada decided to drop the divorce suit. She asked Zee to meet her at Dan-Yee's home to discuss the conditions for her return. Zee was elated! He felt like a prisoner on death row getting news of clemency. Carrying a large bouquet of flowers, he arrived at Dan-Yee's home and, without a moment's hesitation, agreed to all of Ada's demands.

First, they discussed the amount of the monthly allowance for the woman and her two children. Ada, wanting the children to be raised well, told Zee to give the woman a higher allowance than he had been paying. Next, she wanted Zee to promise that there wouldn't be any more children. Ada's main concern was about my future inheritance. If Zee were to have a son by this woman, I would have to share my inheritance with him. Ada also demanded a hefty raise in her own allowance—enough to take care of everything Ivy and I needed. She was tired of hearing Zee grumble about how expensive the children and all their various needs were. Another condition was that Zee provide Ada with a checking account for her Mahjong games. He would maintain a certain balance in that account at all times and, whenever she lost in Mahjong, she could write a check from it. She, however, was not obligated to deposit her winnings into that account. Knowing that she had this money to fall back on, Ada had the added confidence to enter nightly competitions. With her expertise at the game she won far more often than she lost, and since she now entered more games, her earnings were even greater. Ada's final demand was for a piece of expensive jewelry. She felt she deserved it—after all, hadn't she just saved Zee a fortune? After the meeting, Ada returned home.

In the following weeks, jewelry dealers, usually women with bodyguards, frequented our house. Hidden in secret pockets of their undergarments, they carried loose gem stones in little velvet pouches. On large black velvet runners, they would lay out diamonds, rubies, emeralds and jade pieces for Ada to view. After days of considering various stones, Ada decided on a 10.3 carat canary diamond. The gem was then set in platinum to make a solitaire dinner ring. The ring cost Zee plenty, but he was more than happy to pay for it. When Ada chose the gem, it was just a naked stone on a piece of black velvet and didn't appear to be ostentatious. After it was set, however, it looked huge, almost vulgar, so she didn't wear it very often. When, on rare occasions, she did put it on, people seemed surprised that she would wear costume jewelry. Because of the size of the ring, no one thought it was a real diamond.

In a jovial mood one day, Ada asked Zee what his mistress looked like. He said that she was not very pretty. Average at best.

He added that she wasn't very bright and often started arguments with him when he delivered her allowance. Ada had a hard time believing all this and asked Zee to bring home a photo of her. When Zee returned with a snapshot of his mistress, we all looked at the picture in amazement. She was definitely not a pretty woman. Ada, the only one who could pose the question on everyone's mind, asked Zee what he saw in her. Zee then told her the whole story.

At his nightly poker game, the men had a standing order with a madam for eight call girls to entertain them. One night the madam only had seven beauties available, so she sent over an older girl at no charge. At twenty-eight, the woman was considered "over the hill" and was a "plain Jane" to boot. The Madam convinced the men to let this woman pour tea for them so she could have a share of the tip money. After that night, some of the men felt sorry for her, so they let her come regularly as the eighth call girl, hence her nickname, "No. 8."

One night, Zee won a lot of money in the poker game and the men all egged him on, "You are such a big winner tonight, you can afford to buy No. 8's freedom from the Madam. Since she can't attract clients any more, the poor girl has a bleak future as a call girl."

Zee agreed to purchase No. 8's freedom. Once she was free, however, she had no money and no place to go. Again, one of the poker players felt sorry for her and asked his wife to let the homeless young woman stay in their guest house temporarily. After a while, however, the wife worried that they might be stuck with a permanent house guest, so she schemed to have Zee, No. 8's liberator, visit often. During his visits the wife always told Zee that No. 8 was very grateful to him. She urged him to visit No. 8 in the guest house so she could repay his generosity by giving him her body. Since it was free, Zee gladly accepted No. 8's gratitude. Before long, however, she was pregnant. He then moved her to a second-floor apartment of a private home and she officially became his mistress, having two daughters in a row.

After hearing this story, Ada was even more disgusted with Zee than before. She thought he was very stupid to let himself be so easily railroaded into this whole mess. It was easier for her to accept a man wanting a mistress who was beautiful and knew how to please him, than to forgive her dumb husband for getting stuck with a mistress who was argumentative and not even pretty.

Thankfully, however, this situation was now settled and Ada hoped that the family would return to a normal life.

Grandma Liu was a bride
in 1902.

My parents were engaged
in 1931.

The wedding was held in 1934.
Grandfather, father, mother and the Minister of Finance (l. to r.)

Uncle Chi was an eligible bachelor in 1938.

Aunt Jill maintained an attractive figure after her marriage.

Mother wearing her homecoming present—a full length American mink coat. She is standing on her balcony outside of the upstairs solarium.

My giant forehead always cast a shadow on my face.

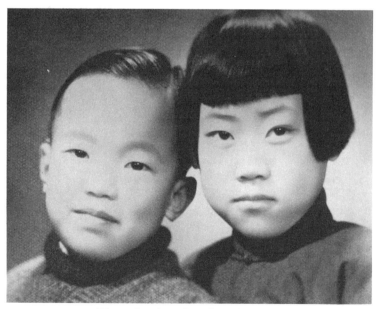

The author (age 5) and Ivy (age 11)

Father became much closer to Ivy and me after Mother left for Hong Kong.

Ivy, Shu, and the author (1952).

I was sixteen, standing outside of the downstairs solarium.

Mother was still fashion conscious at age 50.

Ada sat for this portrait on her sixtieth birthday.

Chapter Thirty-two

After Pearl Harbor, regular air raid drills began and every household was required to have blackout draperies. If any light filtered through into the night, the inhabitants would be fined, or worse, visited by the Japanese soldiers—who inspired fear in every citizen.

There were also random curfews which sometimes were applied to the entire city and, other times, only affected specific blocks or neighborhoods. The Japanese would usually impose a curfew on a particular neighborhood because they were attempting to locate and arrest members of underground resistance forces in that area.

About three o'clock one morning, our neighborhood was completely surrounded by Japanese military forces. All the residents were lined up in the street and each house was searched block by block. Only sleeping children were allowed to stay in bed. The soldiers walked by and carefully scrutinized the people in the street, one by one. Suddenly, a soldier came right up to Zee and stared in his face. He grabbed Zee's chin, turning his head to the left and then to the right, seriously studying Zee's profile. After several minutes, the Japanese officer apparently decided that Zee was not the man he was looking for and continued moving down the line. Zee's face was ashen from fear and, if Mamma Chang had not propped her up from behind, Ada would have collapsed.

One night, our parents were out as usual, and Ivy decided she wanted to go to a movie. She was allowed to go out at night if she was accompanied by a maid. I wanted to go with her, but Mamma Chang forbade us both to go. Usually we were obedient, but on this occasion we really put up a fuss. Exasperated, Mamma Chang finally declared that she would not be responsible if Mother got angry. Ivy was sure we would be back long before our parents got home so, with a maid escorting us, we ignored Mamma Chang and went to the movies. While we were in the theater, unbeknownst to us, it was announced on the radio that a curfew would be imposed on the entire city that night. Our parents heard the broadcast, terminated their parties early and rushed home. After the movie, Ivy and I nonchalantly walked the few blocks home, still not aware of the curfew. When we reached our house, we were surprised that our parents were already home. In a flash, Ivy disappeared into her bedroom. Knowing our parents had already heard everything from Mamma Chang, I didn't dare pull the same stunt.

I walked toward my parents, my heart pounding furiously. Mother looked at me and told me to sit down in a chair. Then, she asked, "Did you deliberately disobey Mamma Chang tonight?"

"Yes," I answered meekly.

"You do know that Mamma Chang represents me when I'm not around?"

"Yes."

"Why did you disobey her?" she asked.

"I wanted to see that movie very badly," I squeaked, my voice becoming a whisper.

"Will you commit the same offense again?"

"Never again!" I exclaimed.

"Do you deserve punishment?" she asked.

"Yes," I said, after a moment's hesitation.

"How should you be punished?" she queried.

"Having my palm slapped with a ruler," I said. This was a common punishment and was considered less severe than a spanking.

"How many times shall I beat your palm?" she asked.

"Three times," I replied.

"Three times is too lenient. Five times would be more appropriate," she stated firmly. I nodded.

"If you commit the same offense in the future, what kind of punishment will you deserve then?"

"Getting spanked ten times with a paddle."

"OK, don't forget this agreement. Now go fetch me a ruler."

I brought her the ruler and stretched out my right hand in front of her. She struck my palm five times with the flat side of the ruler. She didn't hit with much force, so I barely felt a sting. When it was over, however, my mother started to cry. She was strict with me, she said through her tears, because she wanted me to grow up to be a good man—someone she could be proud of. For mothers with many children, if one turned out bad there were always others, but if I was a failure, she would have no one to depend on in her old age. She would lose face for having a bad son. How could she face her relatives and friends?

This kind of teary talk was much worse than any punishment. I felt bad and started crying too, promising her over and over that I would be good from then on.

All through this melodrama, Father sat nearby, reading his magazine and sipping his tea. Finally, Mother handed the ruler to Father and said it was now his turn to deal with Ivy. For as long as I could remember, Mother never disciplined Ivy. She went out of her way to be nice to Ivy, not wanting to be thought of as a wicked stepmother. Ivy, however, from the time she was just a little girl, had learned how to manipulate Father. All she had to do was pour on the sweet girlish charm and he would turn to putty.

This time, Father knew he had to be fair since Mother had already punished me. He picked up the ruler and went into Ivy's bedroom while Mamma Chang got me ready for bed.

Ivy and I had become close, the difference in our ages becoming less important as I got older. We shared lots of secrets and would never betray each other. The next day I asked Ivy if Father had punished her.

"Oh, no!" she giggled. "He told me to cry out a few times so Mother would think I was being punished."

We laughed about the whole thing. Mother was the only one who didn't know the truth.

Chapter Thirty-three ────────

In the spring of 1945, the air raids became much more frequent. Much to the people's delight, American planes were regularly flying over Shanghai. They didn't drop bombs on the city—only leaflets which said that the Japanese would soon be defeated and urged the Chinese people to keep their faith. Many residents would go onto their roofs, cheering the planes as they flew overhead.

Even though it was a crime to have a shortwave radio, people still took the risk, hiding them in safe places. Our friend, Mr. Nu, kept a short wave radio which had very powerful reception. He hid it in a secret room which he had designed when he constructed his house. The room was behind a bookcase. One could only gain entry to the room by pressing a hidden pedal which moved the bookcase. Mr. Nu would listen to the daily Chinese language broadcast from "Voice of America" and pass on the information to friends. We learned from him that the war in Europe had ended and that the planes flying over Shanghai were B-29s, which could fly higher than the reach of antiaircraft guns. To harass the Japanese, the B-29s started to fly over the city twice daily. We could set clocks by the daily air raid sirens, once at twelve noon and again at five-thirty p.m. Even though they were useless, the Japanese always fired antiaircraft guns, and the shrapnel from the guns would often kill people on the streets. Most people stayed indoors during the twenty-minute raids, but there were always a few brave ones standing on the rooftops waving at the American planes.

Summer came and the weather was oppressively hot and humid, as every August was in Shanghai. The evenings didn't provide much relief either. To make matters worse, hundreds of mosquitoes were constantly dive-bombing on everyone's arms and legs. Electric fans were running constantly, except at the dinner table. Ada thought they were too strong for use during the meal so we usually had servants fanning us, by hand, while we ate. At bedtime we all had mosquito nets hanging over our beds which restricted the air circulation further. Every night, Mamma Chang would sit under the net with me and fan me to sleep.

To catch a little cool breeze, Ada and Zee would usually sit on the small balcony overlooking the courtyard after they returned home from their social events. Their bedtime depended on the temperature. Sometimes it was so hot that they would sit on the balcony until three or four in the morning.

One night at two a.m., they were sitting there chatting as usual and the telephone rang. They were startled that someone would call at that hour. Zee picked up the phone. It was Mr. Nu. He was so excited that he was screaming over the phone.

"The war is over! The Japanese have surrendered!"

"Please don't joke on the phone," Zee said, apprehensively. "It could be tapped."

"But it's true. I just heard it on Voice of America."

Still not totally convinced, Zee thanked Mr. Nu and quickly hung up the phone. A few minutes later, the phone rang again. It was another friend who called to report the same exciting news. After that, the phone kept ringing off the hook. Chi and Fragrance came downstairs. People rushed out into the street shouting, jumping, dancing and setting off firecrackers. Everyone realized that this was no dream. It was reality. Tears were rolling down everyone's cheeks as they remembered the losses in their lives. Zee and Chi thought of the old family estate, the priceless antiques and art works from many generations, now gone forever. Ada thought of her mother's death on Horseshoe Island. Now, however, eight long years of war with Japan had finally come to a close. The future looked bright. Everything, it was thought, would soon be, as they said in American movies, "coming up roses." No one imagined then that change more radical and upheaval even more devastating still lay ahead.

Chapter Thirty-four _____

When I woke up that August morning, Mamma Chang told me that the Second World War had ended. Everyone was marveling about the powerful atomic bomb and how terrific it was that the Japanese had surrendered. Within days, Shanghai went through an utter transformation. The streets and stores were decorated with bright-colored flowers, ribbons and banners. All the blackout draperies were torn down and cast away. Street vendors were everywhere, selling souvenirs of the war such as ashtrays and mugs with the names and emblems of the allied countries on them. I bought five flags, one for each of the allies—China, America, England, France and the Soviet Union—to wave out my window.

The disarmed Japanese troops were leaving the city on open trucks. The soldiers sat in the trucks, motionless, their heads hanging low, staring at their feet. The Chinese people on the streets cheered wildly as they watched the invaders depart. Many people ran behind the trucks for blocks yelling and screaming at the Japanese. Others threw rocks and spit on them.

American battleships, meanwhile, were gliding regally into the harbor. People on the street cheered when they heard the American planes roaring overhead, and American soldiers and sailors were idolized. Kids would run up to them and say the funny-sounding word "hello" and they always said "hello" back. I particularly loved the crisp white sailor uniforms. Copies of the uniform were sold at the department stores, and I bought one which I wore proudly.

The Chinese government moved back to the capital, Nanking, and the English and French concessions in Shanghai were returned to the Chinese, finally making Shanghai a completely Chinese city.

The European and American prisoners of war were released from the concentration camps and most of them immediately returned to their Shanghai enterprises. In just a matter of days, it seemed, the French bakeries, Belgian candy stores and all the ethnic food establishments were back in business.

Whole blocks were turned into open-air markets for American war surplus goods, including brown leather bomber jackets lined with sheepskin, Rayban sun glasses, khaki pants and, of course, condoms. The most popular commodities for the deprived Chinese residents, however, were the food items. People purchased butter, powdered milk, canned fruit in large sized cans and especially loved American canned Spam, corned beef, and sardines.

Within weeks, civilian goods also began to arrive. We all went to the open market every day to see what new merchandise had come from America and were delighted with such items as nylon stockings, blue denim pants, lipstick and nail polish.

During the war, the Chinese movie industry had flourished because American movies were not allowed in the country. Now, however, the movies from Hollywood flooded the market, relegating Chinese movies to third and fourth run dumps. Even the pre-1941 movies which had already played in Shanghai were in the theaters again. People rushed to see *Gone With The Wind*, *The Wizard of Oz*, and other favorites for a second time. New movies, as well as films made during the war, arrived weekly. Ivy and I busily dashed from theater to theater, catching all the latest Hollywood films.

This was before the days of subtitles and, since most Chinese people in Shanghai didn't understand English, the theaters usually provided a printed sheet outlining the story line, which you could pick up in the lobby and read before you went to your seat. Later, earphones much like what the United Nations uses today could be rented at the theater. We would plug a pair into our seat and hear an instant translation of the film's dialog.

Betty Grable was the undisputed box office queen of postwar Shanghai. Her movies usually had simple plots which didn't need much translation. A new movie palace, The Majestic, went up right after the war. It was located only a few blocks from our home and, for the grand opening, they booked a new Betty Grable film, *Moon Over Miami*. My whole family got dressed up and went to see the movie on opening night.

There was a jubilant feeling everywhere. Father's business was thriving, and he now felt he could rightfully spend his earnings. To celebrate the end of the war he bought a car, a used black prewar vintage Ford with burgundy-colored mohair seat covers. He hired a chauffeur to drive him around. Ivy and I were very excited when he allowed us to hop in for a ride. Our excitement faded quickly, however, because only a few months later sleek new automobiles from Detroit arrived in Shanghai. All too quickly, our old black Ford looked out-of-date and Ivy and I were embarrassed to go places in the old car. Luckily, Father came home one day soon with a brand new Nash. The four-door sedan was a beautiful shade of green and, to us, looked like it was a block long. It had a radio, heater and turn signals. Once again, Ivy and I thought we were the cat's meow.

Aunt Jill and Uncle Yu returned from Chungking. Yu was able to recover all of his ships from the Japanese and his shipping business was soon back in full swing. He ordered steel from America and, as soon as it arrived, his shipbuilding factory was scheduled to produce many new ships.

Aunt Jill went shopping with Mother and Aunt Fragrance every day. After her long absence from Shanghai, she needed to purchase a whole new wardrobe. The styles of the traditional Chinese dresses the three women wore were influenced by the latest fashion trends from Hollywood. The hem lines were suddenly hiked above their knees and all the dresses sported Joan Crawford shoulder pads. Ada, always the fashion pioneer, convinced Jill and Fragrance to also have slacks and blouses made, pointing out that all the Hollywood stars were wearing them. They also all got new upswept hairdos, making them look like they had French pastry rolls atop their heads. Ivy jokingly called them the Chinese Andrew Sisters. Until that time, Zee, unlike his fashion conscious brother Chi, always wore traditional Chinese robes. The only exceptions had been his own wedding, where he wore a Western-style tuxedo, or when he was horseback riding. He always looked totally out of place next to the modern-looking Ada. One day, Ada finally insisted that Zee order a couple of western-style suits and hired a tailor to take his measurements. When the tailor delivered the two suits, Zee wore them and loved them. He immediately ordered dozens of suits for every season. To Ada's delight, that was the last anyone saw of Zee in his traditional Chinese robes.

Chapter Thirty-five

World War II ended on August 10, 1945, and I entered the fifth grade the following September. Once again I was enrolled in the school I had been attending when I was kidnapped. Now that the war was over, my parents didn't think I was at risk for this kind of crime again. For the first time in my life, at age of ten, I insisted on walking the three blocks to school alone, much too embarrassed to have Manna Chang walk with me anymore. With my tutor teaching me at a higher level than the fifth grade, I found my daily schoolwork to be a breeze and easily made straight A's from the very beginning. I also made friends quickly and naturally.

Before long, I was the leader of my group of school friends. The class president, also a straight "A" student and a very popular boy, had a large group of followers as well. He and I were very competitive at school and a strong antagonism soon developed between our two groups. To settle our differences, my group agreed to meet his group in an alley after school. At the designated time, we all gathered in a dead-end alley and everyone anticipated a fight between the Class President and me. Before either of us could throw the first punch, however, a kid ran towards us, yelling, "The dean is coming! The dean is coming!"

Someone in the class had finked on us. The dean, a middle-aged woman with a very stern face, was marching toward us. There was no escape from the dead-end alley, so we stood meekly and awaited our fate. Before she allowed us to leave for home, she took down the names of everyone who was there and we were all required to be at her office early the next morning. There, she meted out our punishment. An extra load of homework was assigned to all of us. The Class President and I, singled out as the leaders and instigators, were also put on probation. If we misbehaved during the probation period, we would be kicked out of the school.

This was the first time I had gotten into trouble, and I didn't know what happened when you were on probation. Naively, I thought that if I didn't mention the incident, my parents wouldn't know about it. After all, they never came to my school. It didn't occur to me that the dean would send a letter to them. The following day when I got home from school, Mother had already left for her Mahjong game. Father was getting dressed and was also preparing to leave for the evening. The afternoon mail arrived and a maid handed it to him. A few minutes later, he called me into his room and ordered me to sit in a chair. He angrily threw the dean's letter at me and yelled, "Is this the way you behave in school?"

I immediately knew what the letter contained. I started to beg forgiveness, and promised not to break any more rules in the future. Father pulled his black leather belt from its belt loops and began whipping me. I hollered before even the first blow hit me. After two strikes, Mamma Chang flew into the room and threw herself over my body while begging my father for mercy. Father stopped and in silence he replaced his belt through the loops of his western style trousers. If only he was still wearing Chinese style robes, he would not have been able to whip me with a leather belt.

As he left the house, he growled at me threateningly, "Wait until I tell your mother how you disgraced us!"

After he was gone Ivy said to me, "You should have told me about the probation. I could have intercepted the mail for you."

"You could have?" I asked in amazement.

"Of course. I intercept all the mail from my school," she said matter-of-factly. Unfortunately, it was too late to utilize her talents now. All I could do was worry about Mother's upcoming anger and punishment, followed by a long discussion and finally our tears. To my surprise, however, she didn't punish me. She was definitely angry and she did cry as she always did. We had an extra long discussion too, but I escaped punishment because Ivy told her that I had already gotten a belt whipping from Father. Fortunately, Mother thought that was enough punishment. Of course, I never mentioned that Father's first two blows missed me, striking the back of the chair and the third landed on Mamma Chang's back.

After this episode, Father decided that the reason I had gotten into trouble was because my school work wasn't challenging enough. He told me that when I finished the fifth grade, I would have to skip sixth grade and go directly into first year of middle school. He also promised to enroll me in the toughest school he could find.

Chapter Thirty-six ─────────

During the fall of 1945, Ada had been feeling under the weather. Uncle Chou happened to call to discuss investments with Zee one morning, and Ada asked Zee to tell him about her symptoms. From Zee's description, Dr. Chou said that it sounded like Ada had a tubular pregnancy. He advised Zee to have Ada see an OB/GYN specialist immediately. Zee didn't believe Ada could be pregnant and, not wanting to alarm her with the doctor's prognosis, hung up the phone and never told Ada what Dr. Chou had said. When she pressed him for information, Zee shrugged, "Dr. Chou said there is nothing to worry about."

Ada felt relieved since she trusted Dr. Chou's judgment. Zee finally mentioned offhandedly that Dr. Chou had suggested she see a specialist if she was worried about her low energy. Ada always followed Dr. Chou's instructions to the letter and went to see a woman doctor, Dr. Wong, an OB/GYN specialist as well as a surgeon. After the examination, Dr. Wong said, "It appears that you are pregnant."

Ada couldn't believe it.

"Unfortunately," Dr. Wong continued, "The pregnancy is not in the right place."

Ada was wary of Dr. Wong's diagnosis because Dr. Chou

hadn't mentioned this possibility.

"I hope I'm wrong," Dr. Wong smiled. "The laboratory results will be here in three days. Then I'll know for sure. In the meantime, if you have any pain at all, you must call me immediately, regardless of the time of day."

Ada thought that this doctor was an alarmist, but promised to call her if she experienced any pain. Two days later, before the lab results returned, Ada's fallopian tube burst. She was playing Mahjong late in the evening at a large party when the first pain hit her. She thought it was just a stomach ache, which she often had, and didn't pay much attention to it. The second wave of pain, however, was much more severe. As she stood up from the table and motioned for a friend to take over her game, the pain hit her again. This time it was so severe that she lost consciousness. The guests were all very frightened. Everyone was running around, but no one knew exactly what to do. One woman tried to apply acupressure, while others went to find smelling salts. Fortunately, Jill was among the guests and she knew about Ada's visit to Dr. Wrong. She immediately called the doctor. Despite the late hour, the doctor jumped out of bed and told Jill that Ada needed emergency surgery. She then sent an ambulance to pick up Ada and take her to the China Convalescent Hospital, where she met her in under fifteen minutes.

Jill tracked down Zee at his evening poker game. He was needed at the hospital to sign papers. While everyone waited anxiously, Ada was operated on. Fortunately, the surgery took place within an hour and a half of her first pain. Dr. Wong later said that it would have been hopeless if the operation had been delayed any longer. When Ada recovered and found out that Zee had withheld Dr. Chou's original diagnosis, she angrily confronted him, "You almost killed me!" He had no excuse other than that he hadn't wanted to alarm her.

I woke up the morning after the surgery and found out that Mother was hospitalized. During her month-long recuperation period, I visited her at the hospital often. Dr. King, the owner of the hospital, made a daily visit to Ada. Even his new wife made an appearance a few times. Ada's room was filled with bouquets of flowers, as well as dozens of fancy boxes of chocolates sent by well-wishers. Our chef prepared Ada's favorite food and had it delivered daily to the hospital. She recovered quite rapidly and, in the process gained almost ten pounds. After she returned home, she complained that it would take her forever to shed the weight. On her last day at the hospital, Dr. King came in to say good-bye. He handed Ada the hospital bill which, as always at this hospital, was outrageously high. Dr. King sheepishly explained that the bill was for official bookkeeping purposes and Ada could pay whatever she wished.

"I will pay the full amount on the bill except the charges for the operating room," Ada said. "Those I'll accept as a compliments of the hospital."

Dr. King, fully aware that Ada had single-handedly raised the funds for all of the equipment in the operating room, uttered repeatedly, "Of course!" as he smiled and bowed his way out of the room.

Chapter Thirty-seven

One day, Ada's stepmother, A-do, and her third son appeared at our front door. They were homeless, shabby, dirty and clearly on drugs. No longer able to afford opium, they had switched to heroin. Zee, always benevolent, sent them to a hospital with a good drug rehabilitation program. After three months of treatment, Ada bought them new clothes and gave them money and train tickets for their return to Wusi. Zee also promised to send them a monthly allowance. Within days, however, they were back on drugs again. The third son returned by himself to our house and stole a blanket out of Father's car. Later, Ada heard from Aunt Jill's family in Wusi that he had overdosed and died. A-do also came back to Shanghai but didn't come to our house. Instead, she waited for Zee in front of his office building. When he came out and was about to get into his car, she grabbed his jacket and screamed loudly,

"Please save me! You are my son-in-law and the only one who can help me. Please have mercy on me."

Zee was very embarrassed by this ambush on the street, so he gave A-do all the cash he had on him and quickly made his exit. She continued to accost Zee in the same way over and over again for months.

One night the police called Zee in the middle of the night. They said that they had a homeless woman in custody who claimed to be Zee's mother-in-law. She was threatening to jump into the river and kill herself if they released her. The police ordered Ada to be responsible for her mother, so Zee and Ada had to retrieve her from the police station. For some reason, A-do never mentioned Ada's sisters, Shan-dah and Dan-Yee, or their husbands. Once again, Zee and Ada put A-do through a hospital rehab program. When she was ready to return to Wusi, she made a bargain with Zee. She promised she would never bother him again if he would give her a large sum of cash. Zee agreed and A-do happily boarded the train with a hefty bankroll. In less than a month, however, she, like her third son, died of an overdose of drugs.

This was the final curtain on A-do and her family. Ada felt indebted to Zee because of the problems her family members had brought upon him. The worst, of course, was A-do's second son's connection with my kidnapping.

Chapter Thirty-eight

Our family had felt cramped in our town house for a long time. Now that the war was over, Zee thought we should look for another place to live, and leave Chi and Fragrance the entire town house for themselves.

One Saturday at lunch, Zee told Ada that there was a piece of real estate on the market which he really liked and had already inspected twice. It was built in the 1920s and present owner was a department store magnate. During the war, he had leased the estate to the Germans and they used it as the German Country Club. When the war in Europe was ending, the Germans left Shanghai and the original owner got his house back. He now wanted to sell the three-and-a-half acre property because it was much too big for his family. It was located near the west end of the city, considered to be the most fashionable area. Ada immediately vetoed the idea. She didn't want the responsibility of running such a large estate, nor did she like flaunting their wealth so publicly.

Zee begged her to at least take a look at the residence, which he clearly wanted very much. Ada was disgusted and didn't even want to see it, but both Ivy and I volunteered to accompany Father on his final inspection of the house. I was particularly excited about living on a large estate because of my continuing desire for a dog.

Since all of my campaigns to get a dog had been vetoed due to a lack of space, I could see a change coming. We now had a calico cat, who had appeared on our doorstep one day. She was allowed to stay because Chinese people believed stray dogs and cats brought good luck and wealth. I loved the cat and she slept in my bed every night, but I still looked forward to a big yard where I could romp with a large dog.

That afternoon, Father took Ivy and me to see the property. We picked up the realtor and drove westward to the estate, arriving at Great Western Road, a wide boulevard which had three large estates on the north side of a very long block. A continuous brick wall with three pairs of big iron gates, one for each of the three residences, covered the entire block. We were there to see the middle estate. The realtor informed us that the Belgium Council General resided on one side and an American, the CEO of the Shanghai Water and Power Company, lived on the other side. We drove up to the gate and tooted the horn. A guard came out and opened the gate. Just inside, was a small two-story bungalow where the guard and his wife lived. The wide driveway ahead was lined with ten foot-high hedges on both sides. Thirty feet up the driveway, the road turned left and, before you reached this turn, all you could see were the tall clipped hedges. After the turn, the hedges ended and an open meadow suddenly appeared before us. Ivy and I gasped when we saw this huge field, covered with three-foot-high grass. It had been a lush and beautiful lawn at one time but, since the estate was unoccupied, the grass had overgrown. Surrounding the grassy land were deep wooded areas and, at a distance at the end of the property, a mammoth building. The three-story Mediterranean mansion, which took up almost the entire width of the land, looked magnificent, drenched in the afternoon sun. Its orange-red tiled roof formed many interesting peaks and ridges over pale yellow stucco walls, and deep green shutter panels flanked all the windows. We first drove parallel to the house and then turned right to approach it. We passed by a large pond which was stocked with foot-long gold carps. A bridge arched over the pond and led to a small path which meandered up a hill. Atop this man-made hill was a Chinese-style pavilion. For viewing the fish, there was a bench along the pavilion railing overlooking the pond. Many beautiful Chinese maple trees, with their deep red foliage showing, were planted around the pond.

After the turn, we passed under an arbor of wisteria vine and then came upon a cabana on the left with men's and women's dressing rooms and a large raised terrace. The realtor told us that the Germans, for their country club, had set up six lawn tennis courts there. People could enjoy their drinks and watch a tennis match from the raised verandah across the driveway. As we drove nearer to the house, it looked bigger and bigger until the scale of the whole complex seemed unbelievable. The circular drive near the house had tall pomegranates covered with fiery orange flowers planted in the center of the drive. The outer perimeter was planted with orange Cannas, which were in bloom.

Behind the circular drive, a pair of wooden gates led to a cobblestone alley. A two-story bungalow about the size of a normal residence was on the left. We were told that the gardener, his wife and their young son were living there. Beyond the bungalow was the stable, with stalls for four horses. To the right, was the main house.

We got out the car and walked on a paved stone path up to the house. First, we came to the three-car garage and a brick wall, which shielded a courtyard facing the kitchen area. Then we reached the raised verandah. A solarium, which had five pairs of arched-top French doors, flanked the verandah on one side. The living and dining rooms, which were side by side, came next. The immense living room had been used as a ballroom by the Germans, and they had used the dining room as a casino. In the foyer, there were separate lounges for gentlemen and ladies, with smoking rooms attached. The enormous house had a total of sixteen bedroom suites. The master suite on the second floor had its own attached solarium, with arched French windows. From the master suite, a pair of French doors led to a balcony large enough to set up four banquet tables. All of the rooms had hardwood floors, of a medium walnut tone. The floor of the master suite was an intricate parquet pattern. One bedroom suite on the third floor had its own balcony and a red lacquered wood floor. Red had always been my favorite color and, when I saw the bright red floor, I jumped up and down and yelled, "This is my room! This is my room!" After we finished touring the house, Father closed the deal with the realtor and arranged to complete the paperwork the following week. None of us even thought of Mother who hadn't yet seen the place. Father, Ivy and I returned home, elated and full of excitement. Mother was definitely not amused.

Chapter Thirty-nine

Ivy and I were anxiously awaiting the move to our new home, but there were many things which had to be done first. Since it hadn't been occupied for some time, the entire place needed a good cleaning. Also, it was much too large for our family, so we decided to close off the east wing which contained mostly bedroom suites. Next, all the floors needed to be polished and waxed. New draperies had to be hung and many custom-made Peking rugs were purchased for various rooms.

Three large rooms were situated side by side on the second floor, with French doors opening onto a glassed-in colonnade. Father chose the first room, which had built-in glass cabinets lined with bookshelves, as his study, and furnished it with a massive leather-top desk. The next room was made into a game room, and four Mahjong tables were set up in it. The third room, nearest to the central staircase, was furnished as a second living room, because the huge living room on the first floor was too big and too far away for use on an every day basis. Our standard size sofas and chairs were fine for this secondary living room, but all of our furniture was dwarfed by the scale of the main living room. For that mammoth room, extra large furniture had to be ordered. Since Father liked leather, all the new pieces were upholstered in a chestnut-tone leather. The cocktail and side tables for the rooms were done in an Art Deco-style lacquer. Two conversation furniture groups were set up on a huge tea-leaf green Peking rug with a dark green carved border. For the walls, Father purchased many large oil paintings from an art gallery. All the furniture could be quickly pushed against the walls and the rug rolled up, turning the room into a ballroom in a flash. In the dining room, Father had a huge round table made for his poker games. For around the table, he ordered big, comfortable leather arm chairs, all with swivel-tilt bases like executive desk chairs. The connecting solarium was furnished with enough rattan sofas and chairs to seat twenty.

My parents brought over their bedroom furniture from the town house, but their old beds, night stands, chest of drawers and Mother's favorite Art Deco dressing table only occupied about half the space in their new bedroom. To complete the room, they set up a sitting area consisting of several settees and lounge chairs with a large coffee table in the middle. Mother also turned a large alcove in the room into a walk-in closet. In those days there were no built-in closets, let alone walk-in closets—clothes were hung in wardrobes and armoires—so this innovative walk-in closet became an attraction for all her friends to see. For the connecting solarium, Father bought a Chinese rosewood opium bed which he used for his daily nap after lunch.

I kept my big double bed from the townhouse for my bedroom. Mother bought me a partner's desk for the large alcove in my room, where I could do homework with my tutor across from me. Over my protests, she moved three big armoires into the leftover space in my room. After a while I got used to them. They all had large full-length mirrors on the doors and, no matter where I was in the room, I could see multiple images of myself. Ivy got an entirely new bedroom set, with a big brass bed.

Father retained the same guard and gardener who had worked for the previous owners. Before we moved in, fifty temporary laborers had to be hired to help the gardener spruce up the grounds. The trees were clipped, pruned and shaped, and the grass was so tall that the men had to use hoes to cut it down before they could even use the lawn mower. The wide mower itself had to be pulled by six or seven laborers abreast, hitched by yokes and ropes. There were no power mowers in 1945.

Our new residence was finally ready in the early part of 1946. But just prior to moving, Ivy was hospitalized with scarlet fever. She missed the move and, when she finally came home from the hospital, we had already been living in the new house for many weeks. Since she had also missed a lot of school, Mother suggested that it might be better for her to stay home and recuperate until September. Sixteen-year-old Ivy happily agreed. She quickly settled into a life of cinemas, afternoon teas and parties with her friends.

The number of household servants increased dramatically at our new house. We still had the same chef and his assistant, both of whom lived in the quarters next to the kitchen. Another man, a house boy, was hired to run errands and take charge of the first floor. The chauffeur and the house boy were installed in the bungalow with the gardener's family. Including the gateman, we now had six male servants.

Mamma Chang became the major doma of the household, presiding over five maids. Some were new and Mamma Chang spent a lot of time training them. One of the new maids was her niece, Jade. About the same age as my mother, Jade had bound feet. Although women in the cities had abolished this custom long ago, peasants in the remote villages maintained it for much longer. Jade's duty was the night shift. She waited up for my parents and served them late night snacks which she prepared in the second floor pantry.

Mamma Chang had the morning shift. She came into my room to wake me every morning and to lay out the clothes I was to wear. She always included many layers of clothing, instructing me on what to add or take off depending on how the temperature varied throughout the day. Then, she prepared my breakfast, which she made in the pantry because the chef did not allow anyone else to cook in the kitchen. Mamma Chang was an extremely loving person, who cared not just for me but for my parents and Ivy as well. If there was a sudden change in the weather, she would always instruct the chauffeur to deliver sweaters, overcoats, or whatever was necessary to me in school, to Mother at her Mahjong game, to Father at his card game and to Ivy wherever she was. At my young age, I took her for granted and sometimes even thought of her as a nuisance but my parents knew that we definitely could not get along without her. Mamma Chang was so loyal and trustworthy that neither Zee nor Ada ever carried a key. She was totally in charge of everything, including jewelry, stock certificates, gold bars and cash. Without being told, she anticipated our every need. She instructed the maids to rotate our clothes as the seasons changed, determined what went into the cedar chest in storage and what came out into the hanging spaces. She knew how to handle Father's suits and Mother's fancy dresses and furs.

Besides the coat with the stone martin collar, Mother had by now acquired a silver fox jacket, a floor length black cashmere cape with a hood which was entirely lined with white fox and a red silk brocade jacket lined with a furry edge of white ermine. Even Ivy got her first fur—a full length beaver to keep her warm in the cold winter months.

After we moved, Mother's interest in Peking Opera intensified. Her teacher would come as often as three times a week to teach her and Aunt Jill to sing arias. If weather permitted, they would take their lessons in the pavilion over the fish pond. They claimed that their voices sounded better when they were reflected off the water. Father's textile business was booming, and he also opened a weaving factory and shirt manufacturing plant. He could now use his own product, cotton thread, to weave into cloth and then make into shirts and pajamas. With these new businesses, I had a limitless supply of new shirts. Every few weeks Father brought home dozens of shirts for me in various colors and designs.

Father also invested in a plant which manufactured MSG. The Chinese use an abundance of MSG in their foods, so this simple operation turned a major profit in short order.

One night at a poker game, a friend of my father's lost a great deal of money. He told Father that he was not going to be able to pay for the new Buick he had ordered from Detroit, which was to arrive at the dock the following week. Father volunteered to take the car off his hands and when it arrived, sent his chauffeur to the dock to pick it up. We were thrilled when the chauffeur returned, driving up the circular drive in a new gleaming burgundy sedan. Since we now lived quite a distance from my school, the chauffeur had to take me to and from school and also deliver my lunch every day. Naturally, to show off to my friends at school, I wanted to be driven there in the new Buick. Father refused. He wanted me to ride in the old prewar vintage black Ford. He said that I should be thankful I could ride in any car—most students went to school on buses or trolley cars. Fortunately for me, the old Ford broke down one morning, causing me to miss several classes. Not wanting to take the chance that I would miss any more school, Mother talked Father into letting me ride in the Nash or the Buick. I then rotated between the two fancy cars on my trips to school. Grumbling that his family would not ride in a perfectly good car, Father eventually donated the old Ford to the Red Cross.

Chapter Forty ───────────────

W hen the house was finally fixed up to my parents' satisfaction, they invited everyone they knew to a series of parties, with only fifty guests at each one so Mother would be able to have personal contact with each person. The affairs were all catered dinners, alternating between European continental and Chinese cuisine. For more than two months, we had at least three or four of these soirees every week. They were dinners only—no Mahjong, dancing or poker games. Each night, the living room furniture was pushed against the walls. When Chinese food was served, round tables of ten were set up and topped with red tablecloths. For continental dinners, long tables were butted together, end to end forming a U-shape, and then topped with white tablecloths. Place cards were always set for every guest. The Chinese dinners were catered by my father's favorite restaurant. A society chef, Madame Wong, who thirty years later would publish several books on Chinese cooking in the U.S. and become a well-known Chinese cooking instructor at the extension program of the University of California, in Los Angeles, catered the continental dinners. The waiters were always dressed in white uniforms and gloves. Ivy and I were usually not included in these functions—our dinners were prepared by our own chef and served upstairs.

Often, there were some "no shows" among the invited guests and Mother would ask Ivy and me to take a seat at the table. Ivy thought that dining with older people was boring and restricted. Also, she worried that some of the guests might talk behind her back about the fact that she was the illegitimate child from Father's past. Using the excuse that she didn't feel well, she would then turn the invitation down. Since she was naturally fragile, her excuse might occasionally have been true.

In contrast to Ivy, I jumped at every chance I had to join the party. Not only did I enjoy the food, I also craved the attention. The guests usually asked me about my school work and praised me for my polite manners and European table etiquette—not many Chinese boys my age knew how to eat with four sets of forks and knives.

After a couple of months of continuous entertaining, our home life finally settled back into a more regular routine. Aunt Jill moved into a house—which looked like a country cottage in England—only five minutes away by car. She also purchased the first formal limousine I had ever seen—a dark gray Chrysler. Every morning around ten-thirty a.m., Aunt Jill would glide through our front gates in her mile-long limousine to join Mother in their opera lesson, or to make a quick round of the department stores before returning home for lunch.

After lunch, Jill and Mother would go through their standard routine of make-up and dressing. When finished, they might catch a story-telling session before a late afternoon rendezvous with their Mahjong friends.

On weekends, I began exploring the vast grounds of our new residence, with its many hidden areas. I found a large plot of grassy land behind a thickly-wooded area, and would often lie down on the grass and stare at the vast blue sky and floating white clouds. A nearby row of poplar trees looked like they were a hundred feet tall. Everywhere I went there were flowers with different colors and magnificent scents. The only thing missing from this paradise was a dog.

Now that Ivy and I were older, Mother no longer accompanied us on Sunday outings. One Sunday afternoon, the two of us went to a matinee at the Roxy Cinema, where MGM's *Lassie Come*

Home was playing. We rented earphones which translated the dialog and, at the touching moments, we both cried. After seeing the movie, my campaign for getting a dog intensified a hundredfold, and my parents finally gave in. I immediately began to ask for a Collie like Lassie, but there were no Collies in Shanghai. I settled for a Samoyed and promptly name her Lassie. Mother paid twenty American dollars for her, which was very expensive then. Lassie was a two-month-old, pure white fluffy ball with two black eyes and a black nose. She was so cute that even my parents seemed charmed by her. The calico cat was banished to the den on the second floor so Lassie could sleep in my bed. While she was still a puppy, Lassie chewed up quite a few of my sweaters and shoes. I hid, from Mamma Chang, the evidence of her bad behavior in the big wardrobes Mother had put in my bedroom. They were good for something after all.

Chapter Forty-one

When I finished fifth grade in June 1946, Father hadn't forgotten that I was to skip the sixth grade and enter the first year of middle school. Also true to his promise, he found what he thought would be the perfect school for me, Wei Yu Middle School. He had met the Principal and the Dean of the school, who often came to his office to use his direct phone line to the stock market. They boasted to him that their school's curriculum was so difficult that every graduate could be guaranteed acceptance by the University of his or her choice. Father told them that he would like to enroll me in their program and, of course, his wish was immediately fulfilled. I was automatically registered in the first year of the school without any tests or even an interview. Father purchased the text books for the first year the summer before I was to start and gave them to my tutor, who was to have me complete the first semester of my school work during the summer vacation.

My tutor then was a second-year university student who spent four hours each morning, Monday through Saturday, teaching me every subject. From a poor family, he was working as a tutor to pay his way through school. He attended a public university and had a very good academic record. As a tutor, he was proficient in every subject except pronouncing English words. He had a very heavy accent when speaking English and one day I joked about his accent in front of Mother. She immediately decided that I needed a better English tutor. Mother's younger sister, Dan-Yee, told her that the only way to learn correct English was from an English person, and Dan-Yee happened to know an English lady, Miss Coburn, who did private tutoring. I looked forward to my first meeting with Miss Coburn and had visions of soon being able to speak English fluently—and no longer needing earphones at the movie theaters.

Aunt Dan-Yee brought Miss Coburn to our house and we met in the solarium. Miss Coburn, in her late 30s, tall with wavy shoulder-length hair, was quite nice looking. She wore a white silk blouse, a dark gray pleated skirt and sensible flat shoes. To my surprise, she didn't speak a word of Chinese. She and Aunt Dan-Yee were chatting away in English when we came in. Although Mother had studied English for years, she still couldn't understand what they were saying, so Aunt Dan-Yee had to translate everything. Miss Coburn agreed to tutor me for two hours every Tuesday and Thursday afternoons. After that was decided, Miss Coburn asked me whether I had an English name and Aunt Dan-Yee translated the question. Before I could say "no," Mother answered that my English name was Frank. This was news to me. Aunt Dan-Yee saw my surprised expression and asked Mother, "When did he get the name Frank?"

"Oh," Mother said, "he has had that name for a long time."

I understood why my mother wanted to name me Frank, so I kept my mouth shut. Plus, I liked the name. The image of handsome Uncle Frank was still very much on my mind. From then on, I started to use "Frank" as my English name.

Miss Coburn had learned from Dan-Yee that I had taken English in school from the third grade on, so she asked me, "Do you understand what I am saying?"

I could feel my cheeks burning as she repeated the question very slowly several times, but I still didn't know what she meant. Finally, I heard the word "stand" in the sentence, so I stood up. Miss Coburn and Aunt Dan-Yee smiled and told me to sit down. I was so embarrassed that even my ears were scarlet.

After the meeting was over, however, I felt great. I now had an English lady as my tutor and an English name, which would definitely boost my status among my school friends.

For many weeks Miss Coburn and I gestured madly, trying to understand each other. By the end of my summer vacation, we could finally carry on a very simple conversation. Unfortunately, my tutoring with her was terminated then because she was returning to England.

Every chance I got, I would go see a Hollywood musical. I loved the colorful glamorous movies with such stars as Fred Astaire and Ginger Rogers, Judy Garland, Mickey Rooney, Dorothy Lamour, Carmen Miranda and, of course, Betty Grable. These movies were powerful propaganda for the American way of life and the American Dream, where anyone who works hard can become successful. From the first movie I saw, I knew I wanted to go to America one day. Now, however, I wanted very much to learn piano and tap dancing. I mentioned this to Mother and she said she would discuss it with Father. When Father heard this new idea of mine, he blew his top. He growled,

"Are you going to be a song and dance man when you grow up? Musicians are starving to death. What you should do is spend more time on your schoolwork."

He turned to Mother, "Do you know how he gets these wild ideas into his head? He has too much spare time, that's how! He should be learning classical Chinese literature, which they don't teach in school any more. Furthermore, he should practice his brush strokes in Chinese calligraphy."

So, for the summer, instead of piano and tap dancing, I had to study classical Chinese literature for three hours every Saturday afternoon. In addition, I had to turn in two sheets of calligraphy to Father every morning. One day I only finished one sheet and, in desperation, pulled a sheet I had already done from the bottom of the stack. After father looked at them, he handed the sheets back to me. I had inadvertently discovered a short cut! From then on, I didn't have to write any more calligraphy—I simply recycled the pile I had already written. For the remainder of my summer vacation I rotated the sheets and Father was never the wiser.

My schedule that summer was so full and hectic that I was looking forward to school in September.

Chapter Forty-two

In the middle of the summer of 1946, Ada heard a rumor that Zee's mistress, No. 8 had another baby. Before she exploded, she decided to find out for herself if it was true. She didn't want the servants to gossip, so instead of taking one of the cars, she hailed a pedicab and headed straight for the middle-class neighborhood where No.8 lived. When Ada arrived in the area, she first went into a coffee shop across the street from No. 8's apartment and ordered a cup of coffee, giving herself time to contemplate how she would approach this matter. She knew No. 8 lived with her children on the second floor of a private residence and that her landlady was a widow with a young son. While sipping her coffee, Ada saw a middle-aged lady leave the house and guessed that the woman was the landlady. Ada quickly finished her coffee, bought a cake and went across the street to the house. The maid who answered the door assumed Ada was a friend of the landlady, and said apologetically,

"You just missed her. Madame left five minutes ago, but please come in anyway and have a cup of tea."

When Ada entered the house, she saw a boy of thirteen or fourteen reading a book at the dining room table. Figuring the young lad was the landlady's son, she handed the cake box to the maid and said it was for the young master. The maid thanked Ada and poured her a cup of tea.

After a few minutes, Ada stood up to leave, claiming she had another appointment. Then she said to the maid, "Could you walk me to the corner and hail a pedicab for me?"

"Of course!" the maid said.

As they walked to the corner, Ada turned to the maid and suddenly tucked a big bill into her hand, "I would like some information about your tenant upstairs."

The maid's eyes widened with surprise. Immediately, she guessed Ada's real identity.

"You must be..." she could hardly speak.

Ada nodded and said reassuringly, "Don't be frightened. I've known about my husband's setup here for years. All I want to know is whether your tenant has managed her money well on the monthly allowance she's given."

"She manages her money very well," the maid said quickly. "As a matter of fact, she is quite frugal. Why, she even nurses her new baby herself, instead of hiring a wet nurse."

This news hit Ada like a fist in her stomach, but she forced a smile and said gently, "I'm glad she manages money well. Is she a good mother to her three children?"

"Oh, yes, she's a good mother. She rarely goes out."

"I know the first two were girls. Is the new baby a boy or a girl?" Ada inquired.

"The new baby is a boy. He's very healthy and cute, too." This news was a second blow to Ada. She quickly said good-bye to the maid and left in a pedicab.

Ada did not return home that day. Once more, she called Mamma Chang and asked her to send the things she needed to Dan-Yee's home. The next day her attorney notified Zee that Ada was again beginning divorce proceedings. Ada, however, was less emotional this time. She wasn't that surprised that Zee had broken his promise not to have any more children. Though people said that Zee was "henpecked", Ada knew that he always did what he wanted regardless of what she said. The purchase of the new house was one example, and this child was certainly another. Her main concern now was the potential difficulty with my future inheritance because of another male heir. The attorney made it clear to Zee that the only way Ada would return home was if he consented to a property settlement. Once again, Zee agreed to Ada's demands.

In the settlement, Father remained as the operating controller of all the assets but a third of them were transferred into my name. Another third were transferred into the joint names of Mother and Ivy. The remaining third were left in Father's name, the only part which could subsequently be claimed for an inheritance by my father's other son or future sons. At age eleven, I understood that I had just become immensely wealthy, at least on paper.

It took the lawyers a week or two to complete the deal. When all the papers were signed, Ada returned home. For her homecoming, Zee bought Ada an outrageously expensive full-length American Mink coat.

Ada also received all the income on two-thirds of the assets, so she was rolling in cash. She no longer asked Zee for a monthly allowance.

Neither did Ivy and I. To our delight, we got everything we needed, including our spending money, from Mother. She was much more generous with her money and it was so much easier asking her for what we wanted than asking Father. He would always interrogate us about our reasons for wanting spending money. Then there would be a prolonged waiting period while he thought about it. By the time he finally handed us the money, which was usually less than the amount we asked for, we felt like prisoners being paroled. Now, we no longer had to go through that ordeal. After a while, Father only paid for the expenses on the house, automobiles, servants' wages, school tuition and food bills for lunch and dinner. Everything else, including breakfast, afternoon snacks, clothing and bonuses for the household staff, were paid for by Mother. She even paid for Father's English cigarettes and Colombian coffee, our American toiletries, like Ivory soap, and the other luxuries the family enjoyed.

Once again, Ada had been betrayed by Zee and once again she had forgiven him—for a price.

Chapter Forty-three

Zee often talked fondly about how he had raised canaries and homing pigeons when he was a boy. One day, a family friend sent him a canary as a gift and his boyhood enthusiasm was once again renewed. Within a month, he acquired a dozen canaries, ranging from pure white to a deep tangerine color, most of them fancy imports from Germany. The bird cages were hung in the glassed-in colonnade, where the canaries happily sang all day long. All the care for the birds, of course, was done by the servants, but under Zee's most strict supervision. Every morning before he left for the office, he watched the servants' every move as they fed the birds and cleaned their cages. When baby birds hatched, the work was even more intense, requiring special care and supplemental feedings. Practically hand-raised by humans, the baby birds were very tame.

Not content with canaries alone, Zee's next hobby was breeding blue Persian cats. The Belgian Consul General, our next door neighbor, had a male blue Persian who often came over to court our calico cat. Zee decided to purchase a female blue Persian to mate with the gallant neighbor cat. The program was a great success, and we kept all of the exceptionally beautiful kittens. Soon, there were six cats running around the house. Thankfully, Ada put her foot down and had all the cats neutered, so we didn't have any more kittens after that.

Zee also suddenly took an interest in potted flowering plants, even though Ada ordered cut flowers every week from a nearby florist. Soon the house was filled with all kinds of blooming plants, particularly his favorite—all the varieties of camellias. The solarium served as an ideal greenhouse and, before long, it was stocked with many large pots of camellias, which displayed their beautiful blooms during the late winter and early spring. The gardener did the regular watering, but, at least once a month, Zee would sit in a rattan easy chair on the verandah and the gardener and house boy would carry, one by one, each plant over to him for his inspection. Zee would then tell them how he wanted the plants trimmed and fertilized. A couple of maids were usually instructed to hand-wash the plants, leaf by leaf, until every one looked perfect and sparkling. This process would last for up to two hours. When he was finally satisfied, Zee would happily leave for his poker game.

Ada's hobby for many years had been her Peking Opera lessons. Through her influence, many of her friends became Peking Opera devotees and also took lessons. Eventually, they organized a group which met regularly. Each of the members would bring to these gatherings their personal opera instructors, who would play musical instruments to accompany their students' arias. The ladies also played Mahjong during the meetings and, throughout the afternoon, would each leave the Mahjong game to take their turn singing an aria or two. The few who did not sing simply stayed at the Mahjong table. Dinner was usually served around nine p.m. The women didn't sing arias on a full stomach, so the opera instructors would depart after dinner, leaving the ladies to intense Mahjong playing until the wee hours of the morning.

This kind of gathering rotated to our house about once a week. Both Ivy and I learned to sing most of the opera arias by listening to the women. We often sang duets together when our parents were out, but never with musical accompaniment.

That year when September came, Ivy was under the weather again and stayed home instead of going to school. All day long she listened to the radio in her room, particularly her favorite programs which played American popular music. She purchased dozens of song books and learned many American songs. I followed my big sister's example and also learned the songs. We soon could sing "Rum and Coca-Cola" by the Andrews Sisters, "I Can't Begin to Tell You," a hit from a Betty Grable movie, *The More I See You*, by Dick Haymes, and other American hits by Dinah Shore, Perry Como and Bing Crosby. We didn't have a clue what the lyrics meant, of course, but learned the songs phonetically.

One day Mother heard us singing and was surprised at how good we were. At the next Peking Opera/Mahjong party at our house, we were asked to perform a few songs in English for the guests. We lapped up the praise from the ladies, who marveled at our talent. After a while we became part of the regular entertainment for the Peking Opera buffs.

A civil war was being fought in other parts of the country and student demonstrators were filling the streets of Shanghai but, in our house, life was peaceful and fun. Perhaps, as Ada's fortune teller had warned, it was too perfect.

Chapter Forty-four

In September, 1946, I arrived in the gleaming new Buick for my first day at Wei Yu Middle School. There were at least a dozen other chauffeur-driven automobiles depositing students at the front gate. Given the school's high tuition, many of the students were from well-to-do families. The campus was much larger than that of my grade school. It had both a soccer field and a basketball court, which doubled as a volleyball court.

The curriculum was easy for me because I had been tutored in all the subjects during the summer. I didn't tell my secret to any of the students, so they, as well as the instructors, thought I was exceptionally bright. I quickly made friends with a large group of students and took a real interest in volleyball, which I practiced vigorously every day. Remembering my past experience with soccer during my grade school years, however, I made sure I didn't overexhaust myself. By the time I reached my fourth year at Wei Yu, I qualified as one of the first-string volleyball players on the school team.

Each day, I had lunch at the school's dining hall. One teacher and seven students were assigned to each of several square dining tables, and we couldn't start eating until the teacher arrived. Five different dishes were always on the table—two meats, two vegetables and a soup in the middle. The two meats were identical, as were the two vegetables, so, in fact, there were only three varieties of dishes on the table. Everyone also had a bowl of rice which could be refilled as many times as you wanted. Compared to the food our chef prepared at home, the school food tasted terrible. I was amazed that the other students were eating heartily—I could hardly swallow a bite. Of course, I raised complaints at home. Father said that the meals had been paid for in advance for the whole semester. Therefore, it was not open for discussion until after the first semester was completed. Furthermore, it was good for boys to experience some hardship. I then appealed to Mother. I told her that I needed good nutrition and reminded her how I had suffered starvation twice in my childhood. Guilt-ridden, she gave me ample money to buy snacks at the school concession stand. Every day, I bought lots of treats for myself and my friends, and would often skip lunch altogether. Of course, the junk food I bought was not as nutritional as the bad-tasting food in the dining hall. After the first semester, I convinced Mother to give me a large enough lunch allowance to eat in restaurants every day with three of my friends. For six years of middle school, I patronized various restaurants for lunch, and the habit of eating at restaurants stuck with me throughout my life.

We had a half-day of school on Saturdays and, after school, I would gather a group of my friends, pile them in the car and head for home. Friends who had bicycles would come over on their own, and all afternoon a large group of us would run, roller skate and bike all over the property.

The grounds were big enough to keep us away from the house until my parents left for the day. First Mother would leave in Aunt Jill's limousine and, an hour or so later, Father would leave. When we saw his car disappear out of the gate, we all cheered. Now we could really "raise hell." Mamma Chang always made sure that we had enough to eat and drink throughout the afternoon. I made her promise, however, not to hug or kiss me in front of my friends— it would have been far too embarrassing.

When I finished my first semester at the top of my class, Father was happy and bragged that his decision for me to skip the sixth grade was a good one. The winter vacation was only a couple of weeks long and since it was the Chinese New Year, my tutor took his vacation as well. I didn't have the chance to learn my school work for the next semester ahead of time and it proved to be much more difficult for me. I had become dependent on my tutor and rarely paid any attention during class, figuring that I would be taught the same thing by my tutor in the evenings. Talking, passing notes and doodling were my standard pastimes in class. In fact, I talked so much that the teacher moved me to the first row, despite the fact that I was one of the tallest students. At the end of the semester, my grades had dropped down to the middle of the class.

The following September, in 1947, Ivy started school again. She was now in the same grade as I, even though she was already eighteen years old. Though she was never a raving beauty, she was attractive and always had boys chasing after her. Most of them were several grades ahead of her, since the boys she met in her class were all too young. She needed to practice all the new dance steps at home to prepare for her dates and, naturally, I was recruited to be her practice partner. I learned the fox trot, waltz, tango, rumba, samba and the new craze, the jitterbug. Many times, her girl friends would come over and would start dancing in her bedroom with the door closed. Usually, I was prevailed upon to be the partner for all the girls. Before long, I became quite proficient in the many fancy dance steps. Much later in life, when I was a university student in America, this early training helped me get a part time job as a teacher in an Arthur Murray Dance Studio.

Ivy often took me along on her dates with boys. If she didn't like her date or if he wasn't a good dancer, she would dance with me most of the night. We would go to very plush, large ballrooms which had popular weekend tea dances for high school and college students. Only twelve at the time, I was quite a novelty at the dances.

These establishments didn't serve any food or beverages, except tea and cold water, and the dance floor was always jammed. Many of the floors had springs underneath them, which provided a subtle bounce as you danced. One place even featured a mirrored dance floor on its mezzanine. It was important to know how to do the dances properly since everyone was very serious about ballroom dancing, and no one just sat at the tables.

Ivy always told our parents that she was taking me to a movie.

If we had to leave the house before our parents left, she would smuggle her clothes and make-up case to the gateman's bungalow beforehand and say good-bye to our parents in her casual outfit. Then we would stop at the gateman's house, where she quickly changed into her dancing dress and put on full make-up. After the transformation, the next stop was the florist, who handled our weekly house delivery, where Ivy would get a complimentary flower for her hair. Then, off we went to the tea dance without a care in the world.

Chapter Forty-five

The civil war in China between the Nationalist government and the Communist guerrilla forces had broken out almost immediately after World War II ended. In the beginning, the Communist military forces were very weak, but they slowly grew in strength. The Nationalist government, meanwhile, was plagued with corruption, and people were quickly losing confidence in it.

By 1948, the Communist party had enlarged their territory and were waging an all-out assault against the Nationalist government. For those of us in Shanghai, the daily news about the approaching Communist troops from the north seemed reminiscent of the Japanese invasion. Fearing the unstable situation, many people moved to Hong Kong or Taiwan that summer. Ada, remembering how we had lost everything in the last war, began to feel uneasy. She discussed moving our family to Hong Kong with Zee, but he didn't want to give up his thriving businesses. Furthermore, Hong Kong natives weren't particularly happy about the large influx of wealthy Shanghai people, and reports from early settlers who had moved to Hong Kong didn't paint a rosy picture. Zee hoped that a new regime in the Chinese government wouldn't have too much impact on law-abiding citizens. He suggested that Ada move to

Hong Kong with Ivy and me and he stay in Shanghai to look after his business empire. Ada remembered their separation at the time of the Japanese invasion and flatly refused to split the family apart again. This time she wanted us all to live or die together. To insure our future in the uncertain times, however, she persuaded Zee to ship a million dollars worth of cotton thread to a warehouse in Hong Kong.

A typical thirteen-year-old, I was totally unconcerned with the stormy political climate. All I cared about was getting an English racing bicycle. Many of my friends now had bicycles and my best friend, Rick Lee, had a three-speed English racing bike made by "Hercules." I wanted one just like his, but wasn't having any luck convincing my parents. Mother turned down my requests several times because she was afraid that I might get into a traffic accident.

Rick Lee had named himself Rick after the lead character in the movie *Casablanca*, played by Humphrey Bogart. Rick's close-knit family was very westernized and very different from mine. His mother, as a girl, had studied home economics in an American missionary school and had become a devout Methodist. His father, a college graduate who spoke English fluently, worked for the Shanghai branch of an English conglomerate, Scott and Swire, Ltd. Many of their habits were more Western than Chinese. Mrs. Lee would often bake cakes for her children even though they had a maid. The family of four, including Rick's younger sister, Evelyn, had dinner together every night. They even went out to movies and did other activities on the weekends together.

From the time he was ten years old, Rick was allowed to go everywhere on his bike. To me, he seemed to know a great deal about everything I thought was important. He taught me how to distinguish genuine American Levis from imitation ones and, just like Rick, I put American pennies in my loafers. I would buy everything he bought so I could dress "cool." Much of the time, we looked like the Bobbsey Twins.

Mother liked Rick a lot. She hoped that I would learn some "street smarts" from him so I would be safe on the bicycle I kept asking for, and which she finally agreed to buy for me. Father objected to the three speed racing bike I wanted so I had to settle for a regular bike, but at least it was a Hercules.

With a new bicycle in my possession, Father informed me that I could no longer use the family automobiles to go to and from school. My school was only ten minutes away by car but was a thirty-minute ride on a bike. In the beginning, I was very excited about the bike and rode to school every day. Soon, however, the novelty wore off. If the weather was too hot or too cold or too windy or too rainy, I didn't want to ride to school. Since Father was still in bed when I left for school in the morning, I could usually get the chauffeur to drive me to school—as long as I could get him out of bed. He retired very late each night after he brought my parents home, so even though he had plenty of time to nap during the day and evening, it was still difficult for him to get up early in the morning. While I was having breakfast, I usually sent a maid to the gardener's bungalow to wake him up. We had recently hired a new maid and one day I sent her to wake the chauffeur. I finished breakfast and was ready to go, but he still wasn't in the garage. So, I sent another maid. To her surprise, the first maid had crawled into bed with the chauffeur. When my parents heard about the incident, they discharged the new maid, but kept the chauffeur. The Chinese, in typical male-chauvinist fashion, believed that in an adulterous situation the woman was always to blame. There was a saying: "If a man desires a woman, the hurdle is like a mountain. If a woman desires a man, the hurdle is just a piece of cardboard."

That poor maid obviously didn't suppress her desires or put up the proper mountainous hurdle.

Chapter Forty-six

During the summer vacation of 1948, I was aware that Communist troops were marching towards Shanghai but didn't care, nor did most of my friends. In fact, I had the most fun I had ever had. I still worked with my tutor every morning, but Father had stopped asking for the daily calligraphy papers. In the afternoons, a group of friends would come over and we'd play really hard and sweat profusely in the hot, humid summer weather. Mamma Chang always prepared tons of ice-cold drinks as refreshments. Since my parents were out almost every evening, I was also allowed to invite friends for dinner whenever I wanted. All I had to do was to let the chef know early enough that there would be extra people for dinner. Ivy sometimes had friends staying for dinner also, so the house was often full of kids.

The Nationalist government, with its rampant corruption and runaway inflation, was eroding very rapidly. There were frequent riots and protests around the city, mostly among college students and factory workers, and organized, we heard, by Communist subversives. The value of the currency was so low that it took almost a wheelbarrow of money to purchase the daily groceries. Everyone was hoarding gold bars, the only stable form of exchange. Small gold bars, the little yellow fish, were easier to use because of their size and therefore the most popular. Mother was hiding gold bars everywhere. Small yellow fish were laid end to end above all the picture moldings in the living room and the dining room. The numerous Art Deco light fixtures had metal bowls below them which were also filled with gold bars. My parents and Mamma Chang were the only people who knew where all the treasures were hidden.

Totally oblivious to what was happening all around me, I only cared about a collie dog, named Bobby, who was about to be homeless. One of my father's friends was moving his family to Hong Kong and had decided to leave their dog behind. When I learned that the dog was a collie who had been imported from England a year before, I practically flew on my bike to their house. I promised the owners that I would give Bobby the best care possible and return him to them whenever they wanted him back. They agreed to let me take the dog—who was the spitting image of the golden and glamorous movie star, Lassie.

I was surprised that my parents didn't raise any objection to Bobby. Perhaps they liked him, too, because he was so beautiful. I was thrilled to have him and showed him off every chance I had. Most people I knew had seen the movie "Lassie Comes Home," but not a single one had ever seen a collie in the flesh. My euphoria, however, was short-lived. Four months later, the original owner wanted the dog back. His children were miserable without Bobby. I shed many tears as I said good-bye to Bobby, who was shipped off to Hong Kong.

Chapter Forty-seven ────────

By early 1949, the Nationalist government had almost completely collapsed. Many officials had already left for Taiwan, and the army was retreating from the battlefront without a fight. Some of the retreating troops were entering Shanghai from the west end of the city, near our house.

One day a platoon of several hundred soldiers marched through our front gates with their guns and bayonets in ready position. They didn't dare enter the properties on either side of us because they were occupied by foreigners, and across the street there were only high-rise apartment buildings. The servants were petrified when the soldiers first arrived. Father was at home at the time and went down to talk with them. The officers were impressed by my father's stature, but still demanded the use of our house. They had risked their lives on the battlefield and felt that the least citizens could do was give them support. Since most government officials had already left for Taiwan, no one was really in charge of the chaotic situation. Father knew that he couldn't get the soldiers to leave, so he negotiated an agreement with them. They could set up tents on the lawn in which to sleep, and a few officers and women who traveled with the platoon, the "camp followers," were allowed in the living room, dining room and solarium. They promised not to venture into other parts of the house.

Immediately, our servants moved all the furniture and rugs out of the rooms the soldiers would be using, and locked the doors to other parts of the house. The first night, a pregnant woman who was among the camp followers started into labor, creating another frantic situation in the house. The soldiers asked for our help. Mother sent down stacks of clean towels and had the servants prepare hot water for the delivery. Within hours, a healthy baby was born. The next day, the new mother was up and about.

Every morning at six a.m., the soldiers began an exercise routine, jogging and chanting in unison. Though Bobby had already been shipped off to Hong Kong, I still had my Samoyed, Lassie. Excited by all the commotion, she would run to the balcony and bark throughout their program. Irritated by the dog, the soldiers threatened to shoot her if she kept barking during their morning routine. From then on, I had to shut Lassie in my room every morning.

The army stayed on our property for three weeks, and it was a very tense time for us. We had heard many stories about soldiers looting people's homes when they left an area and we feared a similar fate. Fortunately, however, this group left without incident and, along with other Nationalist troops, retreated further southward. The Communist forces, meanwhile, were moving closer every day.

The troops had ruined our lawn. The hardwood floors in the living and dining rooms were also badly charred from the women cooking on them with kerosene stoves. Fortunately, however, when we moved the furniture back in, the rugs covered the damaged areas of the floors. Even more importantly, the hidden gold bars in those rooms, which my parents hadn't time to remove, had not been discovered.

Father immediately hired a contractor to remove our front iron gates and build a brick wall in place of them. Afterward, all you could see from the street was a continuous wall without an opening. From then on, we used the back gate to enter and exit the house.

By April, Communist troops had crossed the Yangtse River, and we knew that they would soon reach Shanghai. My mother didn't feel we were safe, living on the west end near the city borders, so my parents, Ivy, Mamma Chang and Jade moved temporarily to the apartment in the center of the city which had belonged to a friend who had left for Hong Kong. The rest of the servants stayed in the big house and I moved to Miss No. 2's house, which was much nearer to my school. I could get there in less than five minutes on my bicycle.

Aunt Jill and her husband, Uncle Yu, decided at the last minute to move to Hong Kong. They frantically packed a few things and got on the train heading south.

For the next month, I went to school every day as usual from Miss No. 2's home, but my tutor no longer worked with me in the evenings. On the morning of May 27, 1949, Miss No. 2 told me not to go to school. Hundreds of people had been marching through the streets during the night and she thought the Communist troops might have entered the city. We stayed in the house and kept looking out the window, but the streets were totally deserted. The radio only had static, so we couldn't get any information about what was happening. Finally, we started to see small groups of men, armed with guns and ammunition belts, gathering on the street corners. They were wearing very ragged clothes. Some of them didn't even have shoes, but had wrapped their feet with rags. No one, however, dared to venture out into the streets to make inquiries.

At ten a.m., a radio broadcast finally came on and informed us that the Communist Party had "liberated" Shanghai without gunfire. The groups of armed men on the streets were part of the Chinese Liberation Army. They were there to maintain law and order in the city. The broadcast also assured everyone that it was safe to carry on with normal activities.

Young and rash, I hopped on my bike and rode off to school as soon as I heard the news. Most of the teaching staff had arrived by the time I got there, but very few students showed up. No one seemed to know what to do, so I left school and rode my bike to the high-rise apartment where my parents were staying. Mother was shocked that I had been riding all over the city, but almost fourteen years old now, I had no fear of anything. I told everyone that the Communist soldiers seemed friendly. Father, who was never very interested in politics, reiterated his feeling that this new regime might, in fact, be better for the people and the country, since the

Nationalist government had been so corrupt. We all hoped that he was right.

Chapter Forty-eight

The People's Republic of China was officially established in the fall of 1949 and at that time members of the Party who had been working underground surfaced. It was amazing how many there were. My tutor, the University student, was a Party member and so was my music teacher at school. A cousin of mine, a child Miss No. 1 had adopted, declared her affiliation with the Communist Party. She came over one day wearing the liberation army uniform and regaled us with stories about the great Long March. Among factory workers, college students and academics there were many, many more who had waged subversive warfare against the ousted Nationalist government and were now coming forward, proud to be part of the revolution. These underground members expected both appreciation and rewards from the new Communist government but, since they knew how to organize followers and incite riots, however, the government didn't trust them. They had been useful to the Party before the revolution but now it considered them dangerous. Fearful that if these revolutionaries stayed together in groups in the major cities they could become unhappy with the new government and organize protests against it, the government exiled most of them to the countryside. Claiming they were "volunteers," the government sent them to remote areas in the interior of China, supposedly to help develop the backward areas. Some of these former underground Party members didn't survive the hardships en route to their destinations. Those who did live out their lives in places where living conditions were far below those to which they had been accustomed.

When I returned to school in the fall of 1949, it was much different than before. Students were placed in small groups of five or six, with one student as the leader, and academic pursuits became secondary to lessons in Communist politics. Every day, we attended political lectures and rallies, which were followed by group discussions. The opinions expressed by every group member were recorded in a log which was turned in at the end of the discussion. This "political development," as it was called, was carried out under the strict direction of devoted members of the Communist Party.

It wasn't long before this daily brainwashing converted some of the young minds in my school. Students who enthusiastically accepted the Communist doctrine were called "progressives" by the Party members, and they became leaders in the small groups. Many other students, fearful that the report on their political attitude would be damaging, didn't express their true feelings, but it was obvious that they weren't very enthusiastic about Communism. I was in this group and we were called "Lags." The Party believed that we still harbored capitalist thinking and needed to be intensely educated. Some Lags were brave enough to challenge certain issues in group discussion by asking questions, like why the Soviet Union, another Communist country, didn't bother to declare war on our enemy, Japan, until August 8, 1945, two days after the explosion of the first atomic bomb? Or after Japan surrendered on August 10th, why did Soviet troops march into and occupy Manchuria? By the time the territory was returned to China, all the industrial machinery in the region had been moved across the border into Soviet territory. These kinds of questions, which challenged not only the Soviets but Communism as a political system, were deemed dangerous capitalist thinking. Students who had doubts like this about Communism were separated into different groups so each Lag would be isolated among many Progressives.

In the beginning, things were pretty loose in the small groups.

We would have a list of things we were ordered to discuss but would usually play cards, telling the secretary to just write anything down. As time went on, however, the pressure from the Party to take our political education more seriously was greater. We weren't allowed to leave our small group discussions until everyone in the group agreed with the official opinion. Since no one wanted to stay there all evening, we would just go along with whatever doctrine we were supposed to agree to. Before long, even though we were just young kids, we all learned how to be convincing liars. We picked up the lingo we needed to spout to please the Party members and cover ourselves. It soon became difficult to identify the true Progressives from the pretenders, and we all started to distrust one another. Outside of the political study rooms, however, we dropped the seriousness and tension and played, laughed and had a good time like the old days.

Shanghai had many coffee shops where high school kids hung out, but Progressives wouldn't be caught dead in a coffee shop. We Lags, on the other hand, patronized these dens of capitalism every chance we got, wanting to hear the top hit records from the USA, which were smuggled in from Hong Kong and were played continuously. The latest pop star was Doris Day, whose top position was soon overtaken by a newcomer named Patti Page.

New movies from Hollywood weren't allowed into the country anymore so the theaters kept screening old movies over and over, and they continued to attract large audiences. Since kids from Shanghai were the only ones hip to American movies and music, we were the only ones affected by these new policies. People in the rest of the country had never seen or heard them. We all knew that our good times were not going to last very long. Soon the Communist Party "convinced" the proprietors of coffee shops and movie theaters that the capitalist culture was corrupting young people's minds, and no more American music was played or American movies shown. The newspapers claimed that the theaters and coffee shops complied "voluntarily" with the change since the Communist Party never admitted that they made people do what they didn't want to do. According to the Party, people always did things "voluntarily." We students, for example, had to "voluntarily" stand in front of a large audience and recount the evil and corrupt deeds we had done, as well as what our parents had said and done. Since we couldn't escape "volunteering," we usually made up things to talk about. I spent a lot of time thinking up stories which were mild enough so that no one would get into trouble. For example, I would tell the school audience that my parents threw away some leftover food, that I listened to an American record or that I bought some unnecessary clothing, demonstrating how deeply my mind was poisoned by capitalism. I would then be counseled by my classmates that the next time I had the urge to do one of these bad things, I should instead read a little saying from Chairman Mao. I was not yet fifteen, but I had learned the precious skill of survival under the Communist regime.

Many kids, who were subjected to the intense "political education" in school, developed very different attitudes from that of their parents. Older people were often afraid to say what they thought when their children were around, fearing that they would be reported by either their own children or their children's friends to the Party. When my parents had friends over, the guests would usually stop talking when I walked into a room, until my mother or father assured them that I was "okay."

Chapter Forty-nine

In 1950, my father's New China Spinning Mills did very well. The Communist government had allowed him to retain full ownership and had placed enormous orders for new uniforms for the army, to replace the rags the soldiers had been wearing. The New China Spinning Mills was not a very large factory and, with the sudden influx of government orders, it had to run machinery day and night, in three eight-hour shifts. Zee was very happy that he hadn't relocated to Hong Kong. Some people he knew had even moved back to Shanghai from Hong Kong because they had lost all their capital in business ventures there. That colonial city had been forced to absorb several million extra people from the north in less than twenty-four months, and not everyone had been successful.

It wasn't long, however, before Zee's factory was cut back to one shift again due to a shortage of raw material. Representatives of the Communist government visited Father and asked about the million dollars worth of cotton he had in a Hong Kong warehouse. The government, with its excellent intelligence network, had known about this shipment for some time. In fact, it was the reason Father had been given the large orders. Since business was good and orders were coming in, Zee, without Ada's knowledge, decided to ship the cotton back to Shanghai. By the time Ada found out about Zee's hasty move, it was too late. The raw material was already being used in the production of army uniforms.

The government knew that Zee had nothing else hidden outside the country and, once this shipment came back to China, started to tighten the grip on Zee. Government orders stopped coming but Zee was not permitted to shut down the plant or lay off any of the workers. He was told he would create unemployment if he shut it down, which would be detrimental to the economy and the government. Anyone who created trouble or hardship for the government could be classified as a counterrevolutionary and, as such, possibly imprisoned or tortured by a mob. So Zee kept the plant in operation and kept paying wages and overhead. Now that the government orders had ceased, there was no other market for his product, so he quickly used up all of his revenue and reserves. Zee was also hit by a myriad of new taxes. The government taxed products before they were sold and, if the same goods were on hand the following year, they could tax the merchandise again. The tax law was revised often and heavier taxes imposed, which were always retroactive back to 1949 when the government was established. Needless to say, Zee's business came to a crashing halt and his assets were rapidly being depleted.

If 1950 had been a good year for Father, 1951 proved a horrendous one. Every month a group representing the factory workers would charge into our house to demand their pay, and every month, Zee would have to sell more of his assets to raise enough money to pay the five hundred workers their wages. In rapid succession, the cars, the four rental houses, all of the gold bars, the American currency, Mother's jewelry and even the silver table sets were sold. The government, of course, was the only buyer for any of these things, so we rarely got even twenty-five cents on the dollar.

The workers showed up at our house on every pay day for more than five months. Zee had to sit in the living room with them while they pounded the table, shook their fists and shouted "dirty capitalist" at him. They changed shifts every three or four hours, but Zee couldn't leave until enough money had been raised from some deal with the government for the sale of another chunk of his assets. One time he sat there, without food, for eighteen hours. The workers even followed him into the bathroom and never stopped their cursing and yelling. Ada, meanwhile, spent all of her time making the deals for the sale of our assets to the government. She was terrified that Zee might commit suicide from the pressure. Even with the help of sleeping pills, neither of them could sleep much. One day Ada showed me a large stash of sleeping pills locked in a drawer. I was stunned when she said that taking the pills might be the easy way out for her and Father. She promised to discuss the matter with me if their life became truly unbearable.

Finally, Ada sold the large house we were living in to the government. All of the servants had to be let go except Mamma Chang and Jade. Many of them broke down in tears and said that they were willing to stay for no pay. Ada cried also, but had to tell them that the current hardship was not a temporary one and they needed to find their own future. Mamma Chang and Jade were both widowed long ago and neither had a family to go back to, so they stayed on with us.

After the sale of the house, figuring that my father must at last be broke, the government told him that the "kind and generous Communist Party" would do him a great favor and take over the New China Spinning Mills. Father had begged them to take over the business many times before but they always refused, claiming that the government was not taking over any private enterprises. After they squeezed my father dry, however, they eagerly nationalized the business. By then, Zee had no alternative and was grateful to the Party. The Chinese Communists had learned many lessons from the mistakes made by the Russian revolution before them. If they had taken over private enterprises when they first came to power, they wouldn't have gotten the goods hidden abroad or have been able to deplete the assets of wealthy business owners like my father.

The burden of running the business finally came off my father's shoulders but, by this point, he was a broken man. He collapsed with a nervous breakdown, having frequent panic attacks where he would shake all over. He would hear someone at the door and be paralyzed with fear. Each time, we would try to calm him and assure him that everything was all right.

The money from the sale of the big mansion first went to pay off the workers and the balance was used for back taxes. By the government's calculation, we still owed a large sum of taxes, but they knew that they couldn't squeeze blood out of stones.

We were now almost penniless but, as when we lost everything during the war, Father still retained a large block of Success Textiles stock. That company was a huge operation and the government hadn't tampered with it. Amazingly, and to the delight of my father, my uncle and my aunts, Success Textiles started to pay dividends to stockholders. In the beginning, the dividends were rather meager, but later they were large enough for us to live on. My mother, of course, had lost everything too, including the American dollars she had saved for me. She lost all of her jewelry except for two rings she had managed to hide away—the 10.3 carat canary diamond ring and her Burmese jade engagement ring.

We moved into a small three-story town house with only two rooms and a bathroom on each floor. The first floor had a living-dining combo and a kitchen, which was so tiny that two people couldn't be in it at the same time. The main bedroom on the second floor was occupied by my parents. I slept in a closet sized room behind their room. Ivy took the main bedroom on the third floor, and Mamma Chang and Jade stayed in the little room behind Ivy's room.

We finally settled into a less tense life. Mother was thankful that Father had not taken his life when things were tough. We heard ambulance sirens wailing all day long during that period because so many people in Shanghai did commit suicide.

In 1950, when things were still going well for Father, Aunt Jill's husband, Uncle Yu, was not very happy in Hong Kong. All of his ships, except one, had been detained in China, and, naturally, he couldn't manage a shipping business with just one ship. The Communist government then contacted him and led him to believe that a joint venture with them could be worked out. He decided to return to Shanghai to negotiate a deal with them, while Aunt Jill remained in Hong Kong. When Uncle Yu returned to China, the government officials changed their tune and flatly refused all of his proposals. He realized his mistake, but it was too late—the government refused to give him his exit visa so he couldn't leave for Hong Kong again. In great anger and frustration, he died of a heart attack in 1951.

It was a traumatic time for everyone but, for me, the biggest loss was that I had to give up Lassie when we moved from the big mansion to the little house. Father said to me, "in these chaotic times, I can't be concerned about a dog." I knew I couldn't argue with him. I cried and cried as I took Lassie back to the breeder where I had gotten her. Unlike in the movies, I knew that my Lassie wouldn't be coming home.

Chapter Fifty

In September, 1951, 1 started my senior year of middle school. Our life was now drastically different from before. My parents no longer played poker or Mahjong or engaged in any of their former social activities. I no longer had a tutor and without one my grades only hovered around the middle of the class. Since I would be graduating soon, I had to think about college. Ivy, due to her constant absences from school, was now a grade behind me, so she still had an extra year before she had to plan her college career.

I was anxious about what kind of future was in store for me and was quite depressed. Mother insisted on a medical career but, in my heart, I knew medicine wouldn't be best for me since chemistry had been my worst subject in school. With all the adversity she had recently suffered, however, I didn't have the courage to tell my mother that, and add to her disappointments. So, for now, medical school was my goal after graduation.

One Sunday, my friend Rick Lee, who was raised as a Christian, asked me to attend a church service with his family. This was several years before the Communist Party banned religion in China. Being Chinese, I had always presumed that I was a Buddhist, though we had never had any formal religious teaching. After the service at

Rick's church, however, I felt very peaceful. This serene feeling was a new experience for me, and I started to go to different Christian churches on Sundays. Before, I didn't know to whom I could turn when I was in despair. Now, I learned to pray to God. It seemed to be something tangible I could do in a situation in which I was powerless.

The lack of freedom of thought and the constant attempts to control our thinking were the hardest parts of life in Communist China for me. That was much harder to endure than even the material losses and the constraints on our physical freedom. It was very distressing to have to lie constantly just to survive, and I found some solace in my daily prayers.

One day I found a beautiful church, the "Community Church," which had been established by American Presbyterian missionaries. I sat in the front row during the service and felt like I was home. The sermon particularly moved me and, afterward, I signed up for a class for new members and joined the choir. When I completed the course, I was baptized. I told my parents about my conversion and they didn't object. They believed that all religions encouraged people to be good people so, if I chose Christianity as my religion, it was fine with them. Years later, Mother and Aunt Jill both converted to Christianity and became very devout Christians.

As graduating seniors then, we didn't have the freedom to apply to the university of our choice or even to select our major. The government gave us an examination and, as part of it, we filled out an application form on which we could write three choices of universities and three choices of majors under each school. Then there was a blank space on which the "directed choice" was filled in by the government. Regardless of what a student requested, the Party would fill out this space. Everyone was nervous about being shipped off to remote areas in the interior of China, or assigned a major that didn't interest them. The result of the examination and the "directed choice" would be published in the newspaper near the end of the summer vacation.

Mother wanted me to study medicine at St. John's University, which was originally affiliated with an American university. The government had changed the name of St. John's to Shanghai Second Medical College (there already was a Shanghai First Medical

College). I put these two colleges down as my choices and left the third choice blank, not wanting to be sent to some tiny remote village. As my choice of major, I filled in only one—"Pre-Med." When the examination was over in the spring, there was nothing I could do but wait for the news of my fate the following September. I prayed every night that I would be able to stay in Shanghai and attend one of the schools I had chosen.

Chapter Fifty-one ──────────

I graduated from high school in June, 1952, just two months before my seventeenth birthday. I was looking forward to my summer vacation, which I hoped would be a relaxing time without political studies, school work or tutors.

Through the English company he was working for, the father of my friend Rick Lee, had become a member of the French Club, the most prestigious country club in Shanghai, The Club was originally established by French settlers for foreigners only. Now that hard times had come to Shanghai, however, it started to admit members of Chinese heritage. Rick said that his father could fill in my name as his second son so I would be able to be a member, too. The sumptuously built club featured an Olympic-sized pool, a billiard room and bowling alley. By 1952, the Club's restaurant was closed for business. I loved the idea that I would be able to learn to swim and I had seen billiards and bowling in American movies and couldn't wait to experience these games myself. The membership fee, however, was rather stiff for our present financial situation. I still had a collection of American pop records which I decided to try to sell on the black market. Fortunately, the records were in high demand and I raised ninety percent of my membership fee. Mother somehow came up with the balance and, using the last name "Lee" and posing as Rick's brother, I became a member of the French Club.

I was at the club almost every day that summer and had the time of my life. Many of the Club members were serious competitive swimmers and I started training with them every morning. Once, I even won third place in the backstroke competition.

In the middle of the summer, the government notified all high school graduates that we were required to attend a two-week training camp where we were to be "conditioned" before entering college. The purpose of this conditioning, it was clear, was to convince us of the importance of being part of the revolution. It was an intensive brainwashing program conducted by the government to get us to go willingly to the colleges to which we would be assigned. The camp I attended was located at a rural school outside of Shanghai, which had a twelve-foot-high locked fence around it. High school graduates from a dozen different schools were present at this particular brainwashing, and similar camps around the area accommodated every high school graduate in Shanghai. We slept in classrooms, each lined with about twenty double bunk beds. From seven a.m. to ten p.m. each day, except for meal times, we were supervised in nonstop physical exercise, lectures and small group discussions.

The first shock to those of us who were sons and daughters of "corrupted capitalists" was that there were no toilet bowls. Each stall simply had a hole in the concrete floor, with a flushing mechanism. None of us was accustomed to this kind of facility. Finally, one guy figured out a way to cope and taught the rest of us. He looped a leather belt through the old fashioned steel bolt on the stall door and held on to the belt like reins on a horse to balance himself as he squatted. We were all grateful for this little trick.

The next shock was the absence of bathing facilities. Every third day we were allowed to go in groups to a public bath down the street. The weather was steaming hot, always around 90 degrees, and the humidity was very high. The nights weren't much better. After one day of physical exercise in that heat, we all perspired profusely and started to smell. Needless to say, we could hardly wait to get to the public bath that first Wednesday. It was very primitive, but at least we got clean. Our second trip to the bath was scheduled for Saturday but, that morning, we were told we could go home on Sunday for the day so Rick and I decided to skip the trip to the rustic public bath and bathe at home.

When we hopped on our bikes to head for the city on Sunday morning, Rick and I looked at each other and couldn't help laughing—we were so dirty and foul-smelling that there was no way we could face our families. Each of us telephoned home and asked our mothers to meet us at the French Club with a clean change of clothes.

When we arrived at the Club, we made a mad dash for the locker room—which had wonderful modern shower facilities—before anyone could see us. I stood under the shower and watched dark brown rivers of water stream down my body. Dirtier than I had ever been in my entire life, I stayed under the shower and washed and shampooed over and over again. Finally, when we were both thoroughly clean, Rick and I changed into the bathing trunks we kept in our lockers and went out to the pool to wait for our mothers.

This was the first time my mother and Rick's mother, Mrs. Lee, had met. While they sipped their tea and talked, we played in the pool. My mother had never seen me swim before and every time my head went underwater, she would jump up from her chair until I surfaced again.

Everyone had a big laugh about that. Mrs. Lee ordered sandwiches for all of us at lunch time and, after lunch, our mothers left. Rick and I stayed on until five p.m. when kids under eighteen had to leave the pool so adults could enjoy themselves. When we parted to go to dinner at our homes, Rick reminded me to be back at camp before ten p.m. that night.

After I got home, I decided not to return to the camp until the following morning. My parents worried that I might get into trouble, but I was in a defiant mood. "They can shoot me if they want, but I'm not going back until tomorrow."

The next morning I arrived at camp in time for the seven a.m. exercises. Among five hundred students, I was the only one to have violated the Sunday night curfew, but no one said a word to me about it.

The second week's program was the same as that of the first. The only thing which made it a little more tolerable was that Rick discovered a water faucet in the corner of the playground. Except for one in each of the boys' and girls' restroom sinks, this was the only faucet on the premises. Even though it only had cold water, we decided to use this faucet to wash ourselves daily. Each night, we deliberately delayed entering the auditorium, an open pavilion, for the evening lecture. After all the other students were seated, we took our seats in the very last row. Once the lecture started, we slipped outside into the darkness without being seen and, with a stash of towels and soap, washed ourselves under the faucet. While we washed in total darkness, we could see the other students in the lit auditorium in the distance. This daily routine throughout the second week of camp might not have improved our "political education," but it did wonders for our hygiene.

At the end of the two-week training camp, we had to fill out more forms and answer loads of questions. The most important question was whether or not we would be willing to enter a university chosen by the government if it was different from our own personal choice. I answered "No" to that question, stating that I wouldn't go to college at all if my choice wasn't granted. Many students were foolish or brainwashed enough to say that they would go wherever the government directed and those were the ones who got shipped out to the backward rural areas.

The first thing in the morning on the day our fates were to be announced in the newspaper, we all rushed to get the paper. To my great relief and that of my family, I was assigned my first choice, the Shanghai Second Medical College.

Rick was assigned to Peking University, also one of his first choices, where he was planning to major in Engineering.

After the dreadful camp, Rick and I hung out in the pool at the French Club for the remainder of our summer vacation. In September, I saw my friend off on the train to Peking. He had been like a big brother to me through six years of middle school,

Little did either of us know then, the changes the next year would bring.

Part Three: Hong Kong

Chapter Fifty-two

On registration day at the Shanghai Second Medical College, most of the students were dressed alike, in the symbol of the revolution, a Mao jacket. I still did not own one and immediately made friends with several students who, by what they were wearing, led me to believe that they were "capitalist-minded." Like me, they had on blue jeans and penny loafers.

During our first week, we had to take an examination and wait for the school to assign us to a department. We were told that the medical program was now divided into two major sections. One was the traditional curriculum and the other was a newly-established accelerated course. In this special program, students would become doctors in two years. Three days after the test, the results were posted on the bulletin board. My name was listed in the accelerated program under the surgeon division. I was supposed to become a surgeon in two years. "Two years!" I thought to myself. "Who are they fooling?"

Although some people said that the brighter students were assigned to the accelerated program, I was distraught at being placed in that program. I was worried that graduates from this quickie training program would be sent to remote areas of the country where no medical care had been available before. In such backward areas, the competency of doctors was not the primary issue.

Most of my life, as a rich kid, I had expected to have an easy time. I had no reason not to believe, as my Grandfather had always said of me, that I was the "center of the universe and the sun and the moon revolved around me." Now, however, I realized that if I wanted anything in life, I would have to get it for myself. Since my father would not be leaving me any money, I had two choices. The easy one was to stay put, finish my training and work in a job assigned me by the government. The other choice was to leave my family and, like my father had done after the war, go somewhere where I could work hard and would have the opportunity to succeed. I had a lengthy discussion with my mother about all of this. I also told her, as I had in the past, how much I hated living under the control of the Communists. China, I said, was now like a prison to me.

Mother was sympathetic. She said she would help me achieve whatever goal I set for myself, even if she had to sacrifice everything. I decided then that I wanted to live where I could be free, regardless of what I was to accomplish in the future. She wanted a bright and happy life for me and promised to help me escape from China.

For anyone who wanted to leave Communist China, Hong Kong was the only practical destination. Since we had no financial resources there, Mother would have to go ahead of me to try to lay the ground work. Aunt Jill, who was now widowed and also quite strapped financially, had been inviting Mother to visit her in Hong Kong, so at least Mother would have a place to stay in the crowded city.

Father was recovering from his nervous breakdown and was finally able to get out of bed for every meal. Unlike the old days, with social functions all the time, he now looked forward to the family dinner with Mother, Ivy and me. He had become more talkative and even enjoyed listening to Ivy and me telling anecdotes about our daily school activities.

Mother discussed with Father our plan to get me out of China. He thought we were crazy, and didn't have a chance in a million of succeeding. Nevertheless, he thought a trip to Hong Kong would do Mother good. With all the stress, she had aged noticeably.

Success Textiles, the company my grandfather financed, had established a subsidiary factory in Hong Kong before the Communists took over China, and the CEO of the company had sent his son, Mr. Kuon, to run the Hong Kong operation. Since the Hong Kong branch was established early, when China's mainland was taken over by the Communists and all international trade shifted to Hong Kong, it had become very successful. We were still one of the large stock holders in the company, so Mother told the government authorities that she needed an exit visa to visit Hong Kong for a business meeting with Mr. Kuon. She claimed that she might be able to get some money from the Hong Kong operation to pay the back taxes we still owed. Naturally, the government was happy to hear that. They also must have figured that a woman whose entire family was inside China wouldn't choose to stay in Hong Kong permanently. So, Mother's exit visa from China was easily obtained.

Getting an entry visa into Hong Kong, however, was, at that time, extremely difficult. Due to the sudden increase in the population, the Hong Kong government had tightened its immigration rules. As a result, a new smuggling business, with Chinese Communists officials on the take, had sprung up near the Hong Kong border. It was openly called the "Travel Agency" on the Chinese side and Mother decided to use this operation to enter the territory. We worried about her safety, but she assured us that even if a person was caught at the border by the Hong Kong police, all they would do was send you back to China. The Communists, on the other hand, would shoot you right there at the barbed-wire fence border if you tried to leave China with no exit visa or a phony one.

Finally, the day came when Mother was to leave for Hong Kong. I went into her room to say good-bye before I left for school. Knowing that she was making this trip and taking risks purely for my future moved me deeply. I hugged her and thanked her and cried as she left.

Mother was successful in gaining entry into Hong Kong and, after three weeks, we received her first letter. She was sharing a rented room with Aunt Jill and had already paid a visit to Mr. Kuon at his office. He was very gracious in his reception of her, knowing that my grandfather had been the benefactor of his own father and his entire family. Assuming that Ada would probably stay in Hong Kong for two or three months, he handed her an envelope of cash as a token present during her stay.

She then told Mr. Kuon that the real purpose of her trip was to free her son from China and obtain an education abroad for him. Guaranteeing that I would pay back every cent once I completed my schooling, she asked Mr. Kuon for financial assistance for my education. Knowing that there was no possibility that a seventeen-year-old boy would be able to escape from China, Mr. Kuon decided to shower Ada with his benevolence. With a grand gesture, he said, "If you can manage to get your son out of China, I will be responsible for the entire cost of his education. The relationship between our families has a long and deep history, so we needn't mention a future pay back." Ada was very touched by his generosity.

Chapter Fifty-three ━━━━━━━━━━

I was overjoyed when I received Mother's letter, which urged me to apply for an exit visa immediately. Although she couldn't state the details, she said she had been able to arrange some kind of financial help. When Father read the letter, however, he just shook his head and didn't say anything. He still figured that our efforts were in vain.

I knew I needed a very good reason to apply for an exit visa. Mother sent me a letter from a Hong Kong company which stated their desire to hire me. I didn't think that the job offer, however, would be a good enough reason. I had just graduated from high school and had no special skills which would warrant such an offer. The Communist officials would certainly be suspicious and ask me why I would want to give up my future as a doctor under the Communist government. If my visa application was turned down the first time, it would be impossible to reapply using another reason.

Mother then had another idea. She had a friend write me a letter saying that his daughter was very much in love with me and wanted me to come to Hong Kong to get married. This also sounded very fishy to me. I was only seventeen. If the Government official inquired about when and how long ago we fell in love, it would be difficult to make up a believable story. They might also say that if the girl is so in love, then she should come to China to marry me. Together we could build a future under the leadership of Chairman Mao. In that likely scenario, I wouldn't have any grounds to argue with them, so I didn't use that second letter to apply for a visa either. Meanwhile Mother, who didn't know my reasons for hesitating, was getting more and more impatient.

I had been in the accelerated medical program for three months now and had spent more time studying Communist politics than Chemistry, Anatomy or any other medical courses. When we did go through the academic curriculum, it was so quick that I didn't know what I was supposed to be learning most of the time.

During one Saturday morning class, we had to learn how to give injections because the next day, Sunday, we were scheduled to give vaccine shots to the peasants in nearby villages. Our instructor spent about an hour teaching us how to give shots and how to sterilize the needles. We then practiced giving shots of distilled water, first to fresh oranges and later to each other.

The next morning, wearing our white coats, we rode bikes to the farm land outside of the city. We separated into groups of four and set up vaccination stations in different villages. The peasants, who were told that we were doctors, formed long lines, bringing their many children. I tried to act natural, but bit my lip as I plunged the needle into the first arm in front of me. In the beginning we were all rather clumsy and sometimes even forgot to change the needle after each shot. Also, the markings on the syringes were hard to read, so occasionally we injected too much serum into people's arms. As the day went on, it got somewhat easier. By the time we left, I had injected hundreds of people, more than half of whom were children.

On the following Sunday a different group of students went to the villages to give the booster shots and, on the third Sunday, I was sent out again to give the final booster shots. By now, I was more at ease when the peasants addressed me as doctor. I was horrified, however, when I saw their arms, many of which were red and swollen from the shots we'd given them. Some had wounds filled with yellow pus, which were obviously infected. I had no doubt that the future surgeries done by students from my program would be done just as carelessly. Human life, it seemed to me, had a very low value in this regime. Every night I prayed that God would lead me away from this nightmare.

From her letters, it was obvious that Mother was irritated that I still had not applied for my exit visa. Since we couldn't discuss my reasons openly in our correspondence, fearing that the government would read the letters and discover my plan, Mother didn't understand why I kept delaying my application. Finally, she thought that I might have changed my mind, so in one letter she mentioned that she might return soon. Not knowing how to communicate with her, I prayed day and night that she wouldn't give up on me.

One day Rick's mother, Mrs. Lee, called to tell me that the English company Mr. Lee worked for was transferring him to Hong Kong. The whole family had applied for their visas for Hong Kong, but Mrs. Lee was distraught, fearing that the Government might not allow her daughter, Evelyn, to leave. Evelyn was still in junior high school at the time. Fortunately, Mrs. Lee's fervent prayers were answered and both Mr. and Mrs. Lee and Evelyn all got their exit visas. Rick, as a student at Peking University, was not allowed to leave with his family. When I went to say good-bye to Mrs. Lee, she told me that she was keeping the house and the servants until after the new year so Rick could spend his winter vacation there. She hoped that the Government would let Rick visit his family on his summer vacation.

I asked Mrs. Lee to call my mother as soon as she reached Hong Kong and explain why I hadn't yet applied for my visa. I needed a very strong reason, one which would allow me to beg, plead and even argue with the Government agents if they refused my application. The best reason I had thought of was that my mother was seriously ill and needed to return to Shanghai for surgery. I would tell the Government that she was too weak to travel alone. Since Father had still not completely recovered from his breakdown, and Ivy had been sickly much of her life, I was the only person who could reliably travel to Hong Kong to accompany Mother on her return trip.

When Mrs. Lee delivered this message to Mother in Hong

Kong, Mother immediately sent me several telegrams stating how sick she was and how urgently she needed to return for surgery. Armed with these telegrams, I went at once to the local police station to fill out an application for an exit visa. To make it believable, I applied for Mother's reentry visa to China at the same time. Now, the only thing to do was wait and pray.

Soon, the winter arrived. Rick returned from Peking for his winter vacation and I spent a lot of time with him. On Christmas Eve we went to church and both prayed for our uncertain futures. We brought in the new year of 1953 with heavy hearts.

When Rick was due back in Peking, I accompanied him to the train station. We said good-bye without knowing where or when we would see each other again. He no longer had a home in Shanghai, so I offered him our home whenever he came to town. Father and Ivy would welcome his stay, even if I had left for Hong Kong. He thanked me and jumped onto the moving train, waving until it slowly pulled away from the platform.

When the New Year season was over, I resumed my daily visits to the local police station to inquire about my visa. Trying to make my mother's illness believable, I acted out my concern and anxiety, explaining to the agents again and again her urgent need for surgery. My acting got better through practice and some days I even managed to shed real tears.

One day, the agent handed me a piece of paper and told me that I had to get a signature from the dean of my college. I went to the dean the next morning and told him my sad story. The dean was a medical doctor, who had been teaching at the college since before the revolution when the school was still called St. John's and who had studied in the United States in his youth. He was quite sympathetic to my plea, but told me that he couldn't sign the paper until it was approved and signed off by my student group leader.

I knew that getting my group leader's signature would not be a simple task. First, I spent a couple of days making friends with him and, at one point, casually mentioned my sick mother in Hong Kong. A few days later, playing the helpless and pathetic son, I told him that surgery was needed immediately for my mother. He seemed sympathetic so I waited another few days and hit him with the news that I needed his signature. He didn't want to take full responsibility for signing the paper, so he suggested that we bring up the matter at our group discussion. I panicked. The last thing I wanted was to have my visa become public knowledge on campus. Pleading with him not to make this a topic for open discussion, I told him that everyone might misunderstand the situation and think I was trying to escape to the capitalist world. Assuring him that my highest goal was still to become a doctor and serve the Communist Party, I emphasized that I just needed to cross the border to pick up my waiting sick mother. It would only take a few hours at the most. Either my acting abilities had been perfected by then or my daily prayers were being answered—he signed the paper and the matter wasn't brought up for group discussion. I rushed back to the dean for his signature. He smiled at me knowingly as he told me to hurry back to school after I picked up my sick mother. Then I submitted the paper to the local police station and started another period of endless waiting and praying.

Chapter Fifty-four

I always knew that both my parents loved me more than anything in the world, even though I had not been particularly close to my father. He had never shown any affection towards me and was so stern when I was little that I was afraid to be around him. He also never shared food of which he was most fond with us, such as American canned fruit. If he had his fill, Ivy and I might get the leftovers but, most of the time, we would only watch him eat, never daring to ask for a taste.

Father felt very lonely after Mother left for Hong Kong. Though he had finally recovered completely from his breakdown, he had no gambling or social events to attend, so he seldom ventured out of the house. During the day, he only had Mamma Chang and Jade to keep him company and was usually anxiously awaiting Ivy's and my return each day. He gradually shed his stern old self and would now chit-chat at the dinner table with us as though we were his friends. Ivy and I even got bold enough to crack jokes about him and he just laughed good-naturedly at our teasing. Shu, Ivy's steady boyfriend, would often join us for dinner and the four of us had some very pleasant and warm times together. Father took pleasure in sharing with us one of the bottles of good wine he had managed to salvage from the old days. After dinner, we often played Russian poker, a four-player game. Father laughed and joked as though he was at the gambling table with his old cronies. Knowing how much he enjoyed it, Ivy and I arranged for this kind of evening as often as possible.

Naturally, Ivy and Shu were out on dates many evenings so Father and I, alone together, finally got to know each other. After dinner, he would often suggest that we go to the Peking Opera or to a story-telling session. He began to appreciate me as a companion and quit focusing solely on my school work, as he had so much in the past.

In the beginning, I wasn't accustomed to this closeness between us. One night, I was doing homework in my room and Father came in with a freshly opened tin of imported butter cookies. He handed me the tin and said, "Would you like some? They are very good." I was stunned by his warm and caring gesture. All I could say was, "Thank you, Father." Embarrassed, it seemed, by his own affection, he quickly placed the tin of cookies on my desk and left the room. I was so touched that I began to cry. I wanted to go to him and tell him that I appreciated his love, but I was also too bound by old habits. I couldn't say anything affectionate to my father.

I knew that Father didn't want me to leave China, but we never talked about it. I continued my daily visits to the police station to beg and plea for my exit visa. The officers there usually ignored me.

One day in late March, 1953, while I was in school, an officer visited our house. He handed my father the entry visa for my mother. That evening, Father gave it to me and told me to mail it to Mother and urge her to return. My exit visa appeared to be hopeless. "You are dreaming," he said. I felt like a bucket of ice cold water had been poured over me. I could tell that Father was happy, both that Mother would soon return and that I couldn't leave. He wanted the family to stay together.

The visa for my mother was valid for a month. I put the document in the mail and enclosed a short note to Mother, asking her not to return until the latest possible date. I held on to a shred of hope that my visa might still be issued. I didn't know what to do anymore to try to reach my goal except to pray, and I prayed every chance I had.

Three weeks passed. My last hopes were quickly running out, like the last grains of sand in an hourglass. I even stopped the daily visits to the police station.

One day, I returned home after school as usual. Mamma Chang, with a mixture of excitement and sadness, told me that an officer had delivered my exit visa. I started to jump up and down with excitement, but Mamma Chang told me not to act so elated. Father had been overcome with sadness when the visa arrived and had broken down and cried. Knowing that my father had actually shed tears about my leaving hit me like a knife. Mamma Chang said that father had gone to Aunt Dan-Yee's house. I jumped on my bike and was there in a few minutes.

Aunt Dan-Yee and her husband, Uncle Soong, were trying very hard to comfort Father. They had a long talk with him before I arrived, explaining that my future was the most important consideration, and that the true love of a parent required self-sacrifice for the child. By the time I arrived, Father was calm. We had dinner with my Uncle and Aunt and, afterwards, examined my visa. I suddenly realized that it had been issued on the same date as my mother's entrance visa three weeks prior and the expiration date was the same. My document had been held for three weeks because the officials wanted to see if my mother could or would actually return without me traveling to assist her. There was now only a week's time for me to take action.

The trip to Hong Kong required, first, a three-day train trip from Shanghai to Canton. Then, following an overnight stay in Canton, it was another hour's train ride to the border. I had no time to delay. First, I dashed off a telegram to Mother saying that I was leaving immediately. She received it while she was packing for her return journey. Thrilled with the news, she unpacked right away. Her excitement turned to worry, however, when she heard that the railroad between Canton and the border had just been washed away by a flash flood. Had she known the expiration date of my visa, she would have been frantic.

In Shanghai, we didn't know about the railroad breakdown between Canton and Hong Kong. I worried about locating the smuggling organization in Canton, the "Travel Agency," as it was called, to help me get into Hong Kong. Everyone knew I should leave as soon as possible. Mamma Chang packed two suitcases for me that night and I planned to depart the following morning. Ivy, Mamma Chang and Jade spent most of the evening crying. Father didn't sleep at all.

The next morning we all had breakfast in silence. Afterwards, Ivy called a taxi to take me to the station. Father couldn't endure the final moments, so he asked me to wait for the taxi downstairs in the living room. Mamma Chang had my suitcases ready by the front door. As we waited, Ivy just couldn't stop crying. Finally, the cab arrived. I walked to the foyer and looked up to the top of the stairs. My father was looking down at me. We both sensed that we would never see each other again, that this separation was to be forever. With a gentleness in his voice that I had never heard before, he told me to take good care of myself. I wanted so much to run up the stairs to hug him and tell him how much I loved him. Before I could move in his direction, however, he turned and disappeared into his bedroom.

Ivy and I got into the cab. As Mamma Chang held the car door, she started to sob. I had never known anyone as loving and loyal as this wonderful woman, who had devoted most of her life to me and my family. For many years, I had refused to let her kiss me in public, fearing that I would be teased by my school friends. I regretted that childishness and now jumped out of the taxi to embrace and kiss her. She clung to me tightly, knowing she would never see me again. Finally, I moved out of her embrace and got back into the cab.

To this day, I still vividly remember the image of my father standing at the top of the stairs and Mamma Chang's tear-soaked face outside of the taxi window. It was the last time I saw either of these two people I loved so much and who both, I knew, loved me deeply.

Chapter Fifty-five ────────────────

Aunt Dan-Yee was at the train station to see me off. The platform was jammed with people, and the chaos of the situation somehow lessened the sadness of the moment for me. Dan-Yee introduced me to a young woman with three children who was leaving on the same train and going to Hong Kong to join her husband. If I helped the woman take care of her children on the train, she would help me find the smuggler in Canton. As Ivy and Aunt Dan-Yee bid teary farewells, I settled into my seat across from the woman and her children. Soon the train was heading south to Canton.

On the third day, in the afternoon, we arrived in Canton and, along with many of the passengers, checked into a seedy looking hotel for the night. I learned then that the train to Hong Kong had been washed out for many days due to flooding of the river between Canton and Hong Kong. The torrential spring rains had now stopped, but the railroad was not yet repaired. Hundreds of passengers were stranded in Canton awaiting the reopening of the railroad so they could travel the last short passage across the border. Most of the people leaving China were older. There were also a few young women with small children, like my traveling companion. As the only young man in the vast throng, I stood out like a sore thumb. People were surprised that the government would allow me to leave the country. When asked about it, I always stuck to my story that I had to pick up my sick mother and be back within a day or two.

When we first arrived at the hotel, the woman I had helped on the train asked the hotel manager where we could locate the "Travel Agency." She found out how to contact them and I met with my smuggler, who only spoke Cantonese, a dialect I barely understood. Somehow, we managed to negotiate a deal for smuggling me into Hong Kong. The price was $500.00.

I now only had three days left before my exit visa expired. All I could do was wait and pray fervently that the railroad would be repaired in time for me to leave.

Two days passed and I was going crazy with anxiety. Finally, we got the news that the railroad was in operation again, and I would be able to cross the border on the very last day before my visa's expiration.

On that fateful morning, tensely I boarded the train heading to Hong Kong, knowing that every mile of the hour-long train ride would bring me closer to freedom.

As promised, the smuggler found me on the train, but he had bad news. He said I would have to wait one more day because an English officer was stationed today at the entrance to the Hong Kong side, rather than the regular Hong Kong Chinese border guard. The English officer was of a higher ranking than the regular guards and wasn't on the take. This was the first day the border was open after a week's shut down due to the washout and the English officer just happened to choose today for his weekly appearance. Once again, I panicked. I showed the smuggler my visa, gesturing madly that it was the last day I could still legally leave China. I couldn't wait another day, unless I didn't mind being shot at the barbed-wire fence. With our language barrier it took a while to communicate all this to the smuggler, but he finally understood my situation. He said that he would try his best but couldn't promise anything.

The train stopped at the barbed-wire fence which marked the border. Everyone got off and lined up single file to be checked by the Communist border guards. When it was my turn to open my suitcases and hand over my visa, I was very nervous. I had never felt safe dealing with the Communists. Now, I was worried that without any reason, they might stop and detain me. The border guard looked up at me from his desk several times as he examined my papers. It seemed like an eternity before he finally put his stamp on my visa. Next, he went through my suitcases. When he came across a fur-lined parka in the bottom of one of my suitcases, my heart started to pound. I was terrified that he would ask me why I was bringing a winter garment to a semitropical island, especially since my trip was supposed to be a very short one. I prayed silently to myself nonstop. Eventually, he closed the suitcases and waved me through.

I let out a huge sigh of relief when I stepped across the barbed-wire fence. I was out of Communist China, but I hadn't yet entered Hong Kong. Another barbed-wire fence stood several hundred yards away, at the border of the British colony. There was nothing but bare earth between the two fences. As people exited the Chinese border, they quickly walked towards the Hong Kong fence and lined up in front of a small kiosk at the fence opening, where the English guard sat. There were about a thousand people in total that day, so everyone tried to jockey for a position in the front of the line. The people in the back of the line would have to wait for several hours, with the hot noontime tropical sun beating down on them mercilessly. As I had been instructed to do by the smuggler, I deliberately walked very slowly. I stood at the very end of the line to give the smuggler as much time as possible to arrange things for me. I could see the cap of the English officer, who was sitting in the small white booth. One by one, people took their turns and he examined their papers. In front of the booth, a dozen or so Hong Kong border guards in uniform milled around.

Suddenly, the smuggler appeared. He pulled me out of the line and told me to follow him. I walked behind him, carrying my two suitcases. Empty-handed, he walked very fast, and I was having a hard time keeping up with him. I started to perspire heavily under the hot sun. Before long I was at least fifteen feet behind him, but he never looked back at me. The kiosk, with the long line of people waiting behind it, was on the left side of the gate which people must pass through to enter the colony. We were walking on the right side of the line of people. Soon, we approached the gate where the Hong Kong border guards loitered in front of the kiosk. The smuggler walked right past the guards through the gate and never broke his stride. I kept walking behind him as I had been told. When I reached the fence opening, my heart was pounding furiously. I was next to the guards and a couple of them were staring directly at me. I stopped and waited for them to arrest me. To my surprise, one of the guards tipped his head, signaling me to keep on walking. I realized then that all of the guards were on the take. They had formed a wall to keep the English officer from seeing the smuggler and me as we walked through the gate. With renewed vigor, I marched forward.

A few yards later, I was among the crowds who were waiting for their families and friends to arrive. I stopped for a moment and took a few breaths of the free air, which smelled different to me—fresh and vibrant rather than heavy and dull. The woman I had traveled with to Canton had given me a picture of her husband. She asked me to find him if I got across the border first and tell him she was in line. I found him in the crowd and we started to talk for a minute. I had lost the smuggler in the crowd, but he hadn't forgotten about me. He found me, angrily reprimanded me in his Cantonese dialect, and we were then on our way again.

We boarded another train, headed for the center of Hong Kong, which would complete my final few strides to freedom. My Chinese money was now worthless and I threw all my cash in a trash can. The smuggler had to buy our train tickets and, when the vendor came by, I asked him to buy me a soda pop, a luxury I hadn't had in years. The train arrived in Kowloon, just across the bay from Hong Kong, and we crossed the water on the Star Ferry. The experience was truly magical. Hong Kong Island, the "Pearl of the Orient," jutted out from the sea like a jewel and I watched as it appeared nearer to me. I knew that my future was still uncertain and there would definitely be hardships ahead. Now, however, I was free to plan my own destiny. I was free to build my own future, without a totalitarian government telling me what I could do and how I must think. There would be many challenges ahead, but, as I set foot on Hong Kong a free young man, I knew I could meet them.

Epilogue

My mother and I lived in a rented room in Hong Kong for twenty months. We had to travel to Macao, a nearby Portuguese colony, to obtain papers to reenter Hong Kong legally. Mr. Kuon of Success Textiles, who was stunned that I had actually gotten out of China, initially reneged on his promise to help me through school. Mother had to scramble to borrow most of the money for my education from friends and, after a browbeating by Aunt Jill, Mr. Kuon eventually came through with a small contribution. Mother went through this difficult time with her spirits high, however, and never gave up. We would often talk until late at night, planning how we were going to raise the money. I gained a deeper insight into my mother, a very tenacious, proud and resourceful woman. My respect and love for her reached new heights.

Eventually, Mother was able to borrow enough money for me to study in England, and I left for London in November, 1954. While in England, I got tired of people thinking my name was "FRANK LIN," so I officially changed my last name from LIU to LEO.

By 1956, my English was finally good enough for me to apply to universities in the United States. In England I had become interested in architecture and I enrolled in the six-year cooperative program in that discipline at the University of Cincinnati in Ohio. America was everything I had hoped it would be. As I had imagined it from the movies I saw as a child, it was, for me, a place where a person who worked hard had the opportunity to become successful. I managed to support myself during my school years, including working for six months each year at the City Planning Commission, a job related to my field of study and obtained through the University. I graduated in 1962 and then moved to Los Angeles, where I began graduate studies at U.C.L.A. and also worked as a teaching assistant.

Mother had planned on moving back to Shanghai to "live and die" with Father, but I convinced her to retain her Hong Kong passport. I knew that if she returned to China I would probably never see her again. As a Hong Kong resident, she could enter China and stay there for six months. Every year she visited Father for six months, and later, when the regulations changed, she was able to extend her stay for nine months each year. On one of her trips, she smuggled out, in the bottom of a cold cream jar, the big 10.3 carat diamond ring my father had given her. She sold it in Hong Kong and used the money to pay back what she had borrowed for my education in England. Father still collected a large dividend from his Success Textiles stock. He received much more income than he could spend, so my mother always stayed in a luxury hotel with Father on her nine-month stay. With her Hong Kong passport, they could go to any restaurants they wanted and could take taxis, unlike the local Chinese. They were able to travel all over China, and usually took with them large groups of friends and relatives. Ivy, who had married Shu by now, was frequently amongst the entourage. Oddly enough, my party-loving sister had become a librarian, and Shu was a veterinarian.

Many well-to-do people in Hong Kong sent money each month to their family members who had not been able to leave China. My parents worked out a deal with several of these families where Father would pay the people in China and Mother would collect an equivalent amount of money in Hong Kong. Father offered a very good exchange rate so the other families were happy about the deal. Since funds couldn't be transferred out of China, this arrangement allowed Mother to live a comfortable life during the months she stayed in Hong Kong. Mother also managed to send me some money periodically, even though I repeatedly asked her not to.

I finished my graduate program in 1964 and took a position at an Interior Design firm, since the salary I was offered was better than what most architectural firms paid. Two years later, I got a telegram from Aunt Jill, who still lived in Hong Kong. My father had died, unexpectedly, of a heart attack. For me, it was a shock. I hadn't lost hope that I might, one day, see him again. Fortunately, Mother was with him at the time. She took his death very hard, writing me that she was so devastated she didn't want to live. I wrote back, asking her to live for me. Not long after, in April, 1966, primarily due to my urging, Mother returned to Hong Kong, just before the Cultural Revolution started in China.

During the Cultural Revolution, our family lost Aunt Dan-Yee and Uncle Soong, who committed suicide together. Uncle Chou, our doctor and the husband of my mother's other sister, also killed himself.

Mamma Chang and Jade endured many bad times being ransacked by the Red Guards. All their belongings were thrown into a bonfire. They were left with one quilt and one change of clothes each. Being old, sick, cold and hungry, Mamma Chang finally succumbed under extreme deprivation. Jade died shortly afterwards.

Ivy and Shu, fearful of raids by Red Guards, tore all their family photographs—mementos of a capitalist past—into small pieces and flushed them down the toilet. They and their two children fortunately survived this disastrous period.

Father's bank accounts were all confiscated during the Cultural Revolution and Mother lost her source of income. From then on, I supported her. I changed jobs several times between 1964 and 1969 and almost tripled my income. In 1967, I visited Mother in Hong Kong. It was the first time we had seen each other in thirteen years. She told me that I still looked the same. Though Mother was still very beautiful, from all the grief and loss she had suffered, she had definitely aged.

In 1970, I began an Interior Design business of my own with

the most wonderful partner anyone could ever hope for. After a short period of struggling, we were on the road to success.

The Cultural Revolution finally ended and China again embarked on a new set of policies. Mother went back to Shanghai in 1978, and was able to get the Chinese Government to return my father's confiscated bank accounts, plus interest. All of a sudden, she was a wealthy woman again, at least in China. She had to leave all the money there since it was worthless in Hong Kong, where she lived most of the time. She gave Ivy a very large share of the money and also generously divided a large share among the three children by my father's mistress, No. 8.

Aunt Jill and Mother remained best friends in Hong Kong. In 1979, a stroke disabled Jill and she was transferred to a Shanghai hospital to save costs. Miraculously, she recovered and maintains her good health to this day.

I paid Mother's living expenses in Hong Kong, although, wanting to save me some expense, she often made trips to Shanghai where she still had plenty of cash. In 1984, I bought her a condo in Hong Kong, with a state of the art security system, in a brand-new high-rise building. She was immensely happy there but, slowly, her health started to deteriorate. All of her Hong Kong friends were getting older. Some had died and some, very old, were house bound. Since China had opened to U.S. visitors and I could visit her there, Mother decided to move back to Shanghai permanently in 1988. By then, her Chinese money had lost most of its value due to inflation but, because of the favorable exchange rate, my American dollars went a long way. She settled into a cozy little apartment with two maids and a cook. Everyone knew that she hated to eat alone, so she always had many visitors during meal times. Ivy and Shu were regulars. Their two children were grown now and had, like me, come to America.

I spent my vacations in Shanghai to be near her. One day, I found out that with the money I gave Mother every month, she had managed at least in part to support Aunt Jill, Miss No. 2 and Mamma Chang's aging daughter, who still lived in the village Mamma Chang came from. She explained that by helping others, she was accumulating wealth for me in heaven. I made sure to give her extra money from then on.

On December 8, 1993, she died peacefully at age 84, without suffering. I was in Shanghai at her side. Her last words were, "God has blessed me with three wonderful men in my life—my father, my husband—and my son."